SALES IS A CONTACT SPORT

Practical Advice and Ideas for
Building Sales Expertise and
Increasing Sales Production

ANTHONY D. CEFALU

  Milton Keynes, UK

authorHOUSE™

AuthorHouse™
1663 Liberty Drive, Suite 200
Bloomington, IN 47403
www.authorhouse.com
Phone: 1-800-839-8640

AuthorHouse™ UK Ltd.
500 Avebury Boulevard
Central Milton Keynes, MK9 2BE
www.authorhouse.co.uk
Phone: 08001974150

This book is a work of non-fiction. Unless otherwise noted, the author and the publisher make no explicit guarantees as to the accuracy of the information contained in this book and in some cases, names of people and places have been altered to protect their privacy.

First published by AuthorHouse 7/18/2006

ISBN: 1-4259-2139-6 (sc)

Printed in the United States of America
Bloomington, Indiana

This book is printed on acid-free paper.

"Tony...has crafted a grand slam of a resource for sales people and for all who have leadership responsibilities. This fresh wind provides deep and creative insights about persuasion with integrity. It is sure to build reader self-confidence."

Doug Little, Ph.D.
Founder, Great On Purpose
Professor Emeritus
Ashland University

"Tony...brings us back to the basics. Sales is a contact sport. It is an emotional connection... (which) touches our lives everyday. We all are in sales to varying degrees... Tony's book brings out that practical, common instinct we all need to polish. Very innovative and enlightening!"

Beverly Vermillion, Realtor

"Tony has brought the client back into the selling process. So many books preach the craft of selling. Tony reminds us that people are intelligent, have opinions, emotions, and valid reasons for purchasing, or not. Thanks for bringing us back to basics and helping us to navigate the realm of what is useful, insightful, and fundamental."

Theresa Bush, Agent
Insurance & Financial Services

"Sales Is a Contact Sport provides a unique and enlightening insight into the world of business. It is an excellent and necessary read for anyone searching for the tools of success."

Vincent Farris
Attorney at Law

This Book is dedicated to my good friend,

Michael Maple

ACKNOWLEDGEMENTS

Sales Is a Contact Sport could not have been written without the help of friends, family, and professional associates to whom I owe my appreciation and thanks.

Specifically, I wish to recognize the following people for their contributions to this book:

Maureen Cefalu, Lindsay and Tony for their support, patience, and encouragement while writing this book....I love you, "thanks,"

Bernie May, good friend, mentor, and "thinking" partner,

Dr. Doug Little, wise counsel, encourager, and dependable friend,

Philena Myers, candid critic, advisor, and savvy business associate,

Vince Farris, Neil Cooksey, Dr. Richard Parrott, Chris Wogan, and all those who provided me with their professional expertise and personal support to writing this book. I am indebted to all of you and am most grateful for your friendship.

Tony Cefalu

TABLE OF CONTENTS

Part I: Understanding People and Their Emotional Centeredness

Part II: Understanding Value and How It Is Perceived

Chapter Ten

PREFACE

Sales is a Contact Sport is born of the realization that true salesmanship, or the art of the sale, can be mastered by those who understand the importance human emotions and experiences play in each person's decision to buy. Sales mastery comes to those who make an emotional connection, or *contact*, with the customer from the very first time they meet all the way through to the sales conversation and the close. The intellectual, factual, and quantifiable approach and appeal to sales is what the great majority of so-called "sales experts" often refer to as their strategy for opening and closing the sales conversation.

Consequently, sales mastery is rarely achieved. Sales success—real sales success—remains elusive for many even though it is within the reach of any sales professional who learns to understand the customer psyche toward buying and what customers value.

Sales is a contact sport. Those who mix it up and make contact with people on a personal and emotional level move forward in their careers and realize sales success. That is the purpose of this book: to provide a practical and meaningful framework for sales professionals to operate within in order to build marketing and sales strategies that work. Underpinning every discussion is the fact of human emotions and their role in the decision-making process to buy.

This book will introduce you to new concepts of customer thinking that are diagrammed to help visualize what the customer wants and likes. You will also be introduced to a unique way of looking at value and learn what value is and how it is perceived and understood. Additionally, you will be provided with some practical insights into marketing and sales that builds on the foundations of emotional connection and perceived value.

This is a practical book based on a common-sense approach to how people think, behave, and perceive value. I urge you to remain open-minded and personally honest with yourself in light of the concepts that are presented. Nothing contained in these pages has not already been tried and tested to success by hundreds of other successful sales professionals I have worked with over the years. So if you apply the practical marketing and sales messages in this book, you will undoubtedly realize the same sales success in your career and lead a fuller, more satisfied life.

I have written this book with the insurance and financial services industry—the industry I work in and love—in mind. Therefore, many of the discussion points that are presented within are drawn from those experiences. Even so, the principles outlined herein apply to all sales professions and disciplines.

Finally, the ultimate focus of this book is to hold the sales profession in high esteem and to high standards and believes that customers and sales professionals do not operate on a win-lose level. Rather, everyone wins when customer needs are met and the primary goal in sales conversations is to serve and not rule over the customer or the process.

Sales is a contact sport. So mix it up and make contact!

Anthony D. Cefalu

Sales Is a Contact Sport

PART I

Understanding People and Their Emotional Centeredness

"Time teaches all things to he who lives forever but I have not the luxury of eternity. Yet, within my allotted time I must practice the art of patience for nature acts never in haste. To create an olive, king of all trees, a hundred years is required. An onion plant is old in nine weeks. I have lived as an onion plant. It has not pleased me. Now I wouldst become the greatest of olive trees and, in truth, the greatest of salesman.

"And how will this be accomplished? For I have neither the knowledge nor the experience to achieve greatness and already I have stumbled in ignorance and fallen into pools of self-pity. The answer is simple...Only principles endure and these I now possess, for the laws that will lead me to greatness are contained in the words of these scrolls. What they will teach me is more to prevent failure than to gain success, for what is success other than a state of mind?"

OG MANDINO
THE GREATEST SALESMAN IN THE WORLD[1]

CHAPTER ONE

The Lodestar Concept of Customer Connection

People are complex, but they are consistently complex! We all have unique ways in which we wish to buy and be approached during the sales process, and we all have certain ways in which we like to communicate with other people. Also, we all have our own unique styles of behavior and ways of interacting with people given various circumstances. Thus, to say we are complex creatures is without exaggeration. It is a fact of our very natures as social beings.

Therefore, before exploring a new way of selling and developing an effective sales strategy that better serves both the customer and sales professional, we need to understand people more thoroughly—their idiosyncrasies, if you will, and the common behavioral processes that are supported by their likes, dislikes, and emotional needs.

Much of what is discussed in sales training is focused on the differences between people, their personalities, and the ways they perceive the sales process. It behooves us to be a student of these differences and to apply such knowledge in leveraging the sales process to a close. Our emphasis will not be in observing the differences in people per se, but in the examination of those common threads all customers share in the sales process. It is what Carl Jung said about people: They "are different in fundamental ways even though they all have the same multitude of instincts to drive them from within."[2]

Thus, to say that people are different in how they like to be approached during the sales process is an accurate statement. However, it is equally as accurate to say that all people need to and must be approached during the sales process so as to allay their fears and apprehensions. It is from this perspective, the emotional perspective, which we will begin to explore customer thinking during the buying process.

To graphically illustrate the idea that people are emotionally centered by nature, I am drawn to an example found in astronomy and maritime navigation.

In our scientifically modern world of global positioning systems and handheld navigation systems lies a flawless and timeless standard for charting the open seas that is still taught today. Navigation by the stars, as crude and ancient as it may sound, remains the cornerstone of maritime travel. And among the myriad stars in the night sky that are used to point ships in the right direction, there is a single bright point that stands out among the dark backdrop of the speckled night sky: a reference star, or lodestar, used as a sure guide, infallible in its reliability. It is a constant by which all other stars revolve around when viewed from an earthly perspective.

By name, it is Polaris, or the North Star. It is a star located at the end of the handle of the Little Dipper. If one were to stand at the North Pole and look straight up from a spinning earth, one star would appear as if all other stars in the sky were orbiting about it. That would be Polaris, the North Star, the navigators' lodestar of reference and direction.

So, at any time in the night and at any place on the globe, if you find the North Star, the lodestar, you will be able to chart your course accurately and successfully to your destination. If you get lost, just look up, find the lodestar of the north, and you will find your way. It is there for all to see, reliable, constant, a fundamental and unchanging truth, a guide to those who are trained to look for it and use it. This idea brings us to the foundational theory and guide about people and buying called the Lodestar Concept of Customer Connection.

The Lodestar Concept of Customer Connection helps you, the sales professional, to visualize, at a glance, not only the complex nature of people, but their general and common nature as well. It is a graphic guide to navigating the waters of the sales process and to building sales habits that successfully move the customer to buy and stay with you as a client.

Fundamental to sales success is a thorough understanding of how customers define and perceive value. In the following chapters, I will explain the mental process they go through when buying. Each point of the star will be examined in light of the single most important constant to understanding that process which is: Buying is never an emotionally neutral event for people.

In fact, all sales and business transactions have at their core emotions that drive customer behavior. On the periphery of that core is a veneer of logic and rationality that supports the emotional core of our natures. Understand this constant of human behavior and you are well on your way to sales expertise and sales success.

CHAPTER ONE: KEY NOTES

The Lodestar Concept of Customer Connection

*   <u>People are complex, but they are consistently complex!</u> As social beings, we "crave" connection emotionally with other people. In that respect, we are complex, but we are consistently complex.

*   <u>People are emotionally centered.</u> This point is graphically depicted by the lodestar graphic. People use logic in making decisions. But it is emotion that first drives people to decide, to buy, to act and to do something.

*   <u>The Lodestar Concept of Customer Connection</u> gives a trained eye to the nature of people and graphically illustrates the core makeup of human nature. That core makeup is our emotional centeredness and how we predominantly react and make decisions based off of emotion and justify later with logic.

The Lodestar Concept of Customer Connection

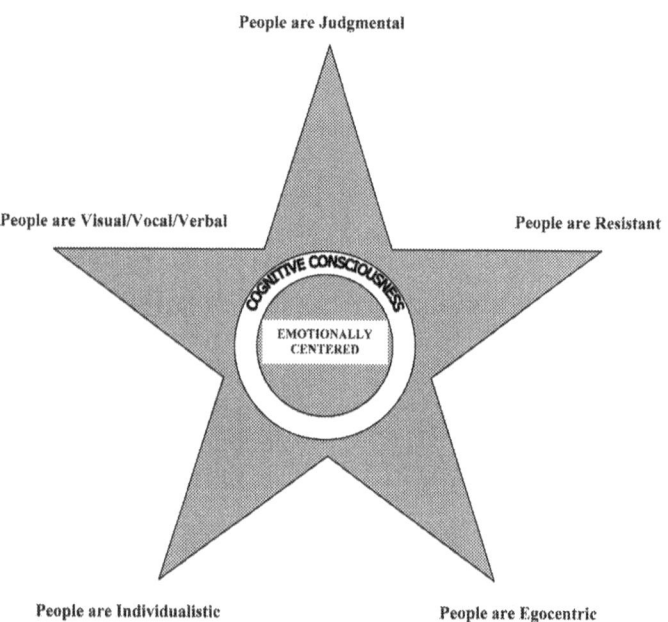

People are Judgmental

People are Visual/Vocal/Verbal

People are Resistant

COGNITIVE CONSCIOUSNESS

EMOTIONALLY CENTERED

People are Individualistic

People are Egocentric

> *"As rational human beings, we like to think that logic drives most of our decisions. But the fact is, in most persuasive situations, people buy on emotion and justify with fact. People may be persuaded by reason, but they are moved by emotion."*

Harry Mills
Artful Persuasion[1]

CHAPTER TWO
People Are Emotionally Centered

People are emotional creatures. Yes, logic does play an important role in our day-to-day ability to function and think. But it is our emotions that drive us to decide, to act, to choose or not to choose, to respond to the situation at hand. In the sales arena, it is our emotional nature that overrides all else in moving us to buy—not logic and not the cold, cruel facts of product features and service offers. It is our emotions that rule the day.

"All emotions are, in essence, impulses to act, the instant plans for handling life that evolution has instilled in us. The very root of the word emotion is motere, the Latin verb "to move," plus the prefix "e-" to connote "move away," suggesting that a tendency to act is implicit in every emotion."

DANIEL GOLEMAN
EMOTIONAL INTELLIGENCE [2]

Those emotional impulses to act that Daniel Goleman refers to are wrapped in a cognitive consciousness we call "logic" or "rational awareness." This is an area of the mind that deals only with the facts of things. It is at this cognitive conscious level or logical realm of our minds that we support the emotional motives for decision-making, or as Goleman says, our "tendency to act."

I refer to it as being "logically dispersed" in our thinking and decision-making process to buy. Logic is dispersed throughout our thinking and is used selectively to support the emotional decision to buy. In other words, we disperse facts and rational thought whenever there is a need to justify the emotional motives for buying something.

For example, I buy a red sports car for fun and the appeal it has in making me feel youthful and successful; I justify it logically to my wife that it was a good purchase price, a once-in-a-lifetime deal, and that we will save money in the long run because it is great on gas. I know it is weak logic...but it is logic nonetheless. We go through this emotionally centered, logically dispersed cycle every time we purchase something.

Harry Mills, author of twenty-two books on sales, negotiation, and influence and whose clients include IBM, PricewaterhouseCoopers, KPMG, Ernst & Young, Lexus, and Toyota states, "As rational human beings, we like to think that logic drives most of our decisions. But the fact is, in most persuasive situations, people buy on emotion and justify with fact. People may be persuaded by reason, but they are moved by emotion."

It is emotion that causes us to drop our natural defenses and distracts us from the sales expert's intention to persuade. It is emotion that requires less effort to process mentally than logical thought or argument. It takes more mental effort to process facts than it does an emotional appeal. Emotional stories are more interesting than facts. Emotional contact through imagery, music, vocals are all much easier to recall than factual evidence. Emotions rule. Why? The reason is because we are emotionally centered creatures by nature.[3]

That is not to say that logic, the cognitive consciousness, is divorced of the emotional connection and our ability to act or decide. In fact, logic and emotion are intertwined. They are partners that are dependent upon one another, jointly affecting the overall impulse to buy. But it is the emotional center that exerts the greatest force on our urge to purchase something.

Scientifically, the evidence is overwhelming as to the fact of our emotionally centered nature and its link to act, to decide and to buy. Research that began over 150 years ago examined the relationships between emotions and reasoning skills. The ability to act and decide is lost when areas of the brain that govern emotion are damaged through accident or illness.[4]

Dr. Antonio Damasio, neurologist from the University of Iowa College of Medicine, completed and published a study in 1994 confirming that patients with damage to the emotional triggers within the brain demonstrate "terribly flawed" decision-making ability yet they show no deterioration in IQ or cognitive ability. "Despite their intact intelligence," Dr. Damasio states, "they make disastrous choices in business and their personal lives and can even obsess endlessly over a decision so simple as when to make an appointment."[5]

Emotionally Centered and Logically Dispersed

When our passions, or emotions, are aroused, the emotional side holds the rational in check, insinuating itself in precedence and importance in the decision-making process. We are simply "hardwired" this way through a fast-track neural network where rational thought runs indirectly connected with the body's functions.

Emotions actually stimulate the mind three thousand times faster than regular thought, verifying that in most situations, emotions move a person to act faster than rational thought ever could.[6] This is one of the underlying reasons why our choices are based on approximately 80%

emotion (Emotionally Centered) and 20% on selective logic (Cognitive Consciousness).

"When dealing with people, remember you are not dealing with creatures of logic, but with creatures of emotion, creatures bristling with prejudice and motivated by pride and vanity."

DALE CARNEGIE
HOW TO WIN FRIENDS AND INFLUENCE PEOPLE[7]

We are logically dispersed, first of all, because our rational thinking (logic) is not at the core of our natures; emotions are at our core, and logic is thus dispersed out from the decision-making process.

Secondly, we are emotionally centered and logically dispersed because of the way in which logic is used to support the emotional decision to decide and act. Logic is used only to the extent that it supports the emotional decision to buy or act. In other words, the use of logic is scattered (dispersed); it only becomes relevant and useful at various points in order to justify an emotional decision or act, such as the decision to buy something.

I like to illustrate the fact of our emotional centeredness by placing emotions in the heart of the lodestar graphic. Yet, surrounding that emotionally centered core is a shell, the cognitive consciousness. That is the rational, quantitative, aware, and ever-present side of the mind that is in-touch and engaged with the surrounding environment.

Notice that the dominant feature is the emotional core, the preeminent factor in all decisions that are made. The two, the emotional core and the conscious cognitive shell, are inseparable, partnering together in this dominant-recessive relationship in order to make "good choices."

Again, emotions rule, and the fact remains constant that we are emotionally centered creatures that are logically dispersed in our thinking and abilities to act and decide on things.

Finally, it is a well-known fact that the physiology of our brain is divided into two clear and distinct hemispheres. Although connected, the two hemispheres possess separate functions and traits.

The left side is the quantitative side of our thinking. It is detail-seeking, rational, factual, and analytical in its processing and understanding. It is the rules and regulations side of our mind that crunches the numbers, counts the "debits and credits," plans each step, organizes into parts, reasons logically and puts things in their literal context. It is triggered by information and gives place to the quantifiable. It is stirred by statistics and satiated with a diet of facts, figures, and data.

On the other hand, the right side of the brain is that part of the mind that puts each piece together; forms pictures; gets a feeling; and is stirred by stories, visuals, humor, and vocals. It understands the meaning and relevance of things. It is the conceptual side of the brain where beliefs, hope, and intuition reside. And, as a matter of fact, it is also the seat of our emotional centeredness and instinct and our urge to decide to act on something.

Once we understand this point—that our emotional selves and decision-making abilities are right-brain functions—we, as sales experts, "will immediately see the relevance of learning to speak the language of the right brain," both literally in our sales discussions and practically in our marketing and sales strategies.[8]

Don't Be a Half-Brained Sales Professional

Don't be the kind of sales professional that is always trying to appeal to the logic of the left brain when speaking to customers. Be in your right mind, stimulate the customer's emotions, and understand their emotional centeredness for what it is—the natural and dominant factor triggering the customer's impulse to buy. I am not talking about sales manipulation. That is an entirely different thing and a concept I wholly reject. I am talking about being a complete sales expert—one who uses logic, reason, and accurate data and features to support the emotional criteria of why someone would buy a product or service for themselves.

In the industry I work in—the insurance and financial services industry—part of our product portfolio includes life insurance in order to meet our customer's needs. Therefore, incorporated into our sales conversations is a systematic fact-finding process for analyzing a customer's insurance and financial situation and making helpful recommendations to improve it.

In the final analysis, we come up with a number, a monetary life insurance need for example. Alone, it is a cold, hard, cruel, in-your-face dollar amount that tells the customer what they need in order to secure their family's financial future.

Now, the sad thing is that most salespeople go through the analysis flawlessly. They ask the necessary questions, they analyze the numbers, and viola! A number is derived demonstrating conclusively what the customer needs in order to protect their family.

For example, after going through the analysis process a customer need for $300,000 in additional life insurance is identified. And what happens in such situations, more often than it should, is that the customer walks away in shock, needing to "think about it" versus getting the protection you know they need and they know they need.

Bert Decker, a leader and expert in how to communicate says, "If you want to influence, persuade, or motivate people, you have to make emotional contact with them."[9]

Sales Is a Contact Sport!

All the facts, all the logic, all the rational reasons for buying something are vain unless we make contact emotionally with the customer. It is not the "what it is" that closes the sale and prompts the customer to buy; it is the "what it does" for them in meeting an emotional reason or need for buying that moves them to action. I call that the "emotional criteria" for buying.

"Action springs out of what we fundamentally desire...and the best piece of advice which can be given to would-be persuaders, whether in business, in the home, in the school, in politics, is: First, arouse in the other person an eager want. He who can do this has the whole world with him. He who cannot walks a lonely way."

HARRY A. OVERSTREET
INFLUENCING HUMAN BEHAVIOR[10]

Returning to our example, it is not enough to stimulate the left brain by telling a customer that they have a need of $300,000 in life insurance. The customer must also be stimulated in the right brain where imagery, metaphors, stories, and the specific emotional criteria for why the customer would buy in the first place reside. The number or dollar amount alone is benign, unemotional and weak in its ability to stimulate the customer into action--into the action of buying.

With life insurance, I can tell the customer the differences between term and whole life, or the interest-bearing advantages of universal life and variable products. That is all very important for the customer to know. But, often, these facts are over communicated or are the only aspect of the sales conversation communicated with the customer. As a result, such left brain sales conversations leave the stirring of emotion, and thus, the impulse to buy a weak proposition for the customer.

Uncover what it is they really want out of the product. Ask good questions of the customer; confirm the numbers to meet their need. With this approach, what they want their life insurance program to do for them is, in essence, their emotional reason or criteria for buying.

The answer to "why" a customer is looking to buy or "what" it is they want to get or accomplish through purchasing a product provides the sales professional with the verbiage necessary to accompany the $300,000 life insurance need. It may be that the customer desires to keep a promise of providing for a child's college education. It may be that they wish to preserve the lifestyle they have worked so hard to provide for their family and loved ones. Or perhaps they want to use it to pay the estate taxes so the family farm isn't at risk of being "cut up" or sold off piecemeal in order to pay government taxes.

Whatever the emotional criteria for wanting to buy, the sales expert must uncover it in order to present the most compelling reason (right-brain stimulus) to the customer for buying.

Sales pioneer and insurance legend, Ben Feldman of East Liverpool, Ohio, sought the customer's emotional reason for buying through a strategy he called the "disturbing question." He would ask the hard questions of people, the emotional questions, the questions that struck at the heart and core of what people face, and pointed out how we, in the insurance industry, could assist them in avoiding or minimizing the risks that they face every day.

In the insurance and financial services industry, this is the one critical skill that separates the "good" from the "great" sales professionals.

In the following chapters, we will take a closer look at the customer and the issues surrounding emotional centeredness and the idea that people are logically dispersed. We will look at how customers are judgmental; egocentric; naturally resistant, individualistic in their thinking, and how they are visual, vocal, and verbal in how they connect with other people.

In turn, your newfound understanding of the facts of human behavior and emotional tendencies will help you to formulate practical strategies that are focused on gaining emotional connection during the sales process and that help you build your customer base.

This knowledge will also help you to retain your customers and build in-office and even company-wide strategies where emotional connection and positive experiences are found at every juncture of contact.

And, finally, your knowledge of emotional centeredness will help you to build strategies that touch customers and speak of added value for them.

If you understand all that there is about the emotional centeredness of the customer, you will be able to construct a marketing model and a sales system that effectively defines value in terms the customer will understand, appreciate, and connect with.

"Customers are not always right. They make mistakes; they forget things; they get confused. But customers are always emotional."

JANNELLE BARLOW AND DIANNA MAUL
EMOTIONAL VALUE[11]

CHAPTER TWO: KEY NOTES

People Are Emotionally Centered

*   <u>Impulses to act and decide to buy are emotionally based.</u> The very core of our nature is to act and be emotional. People may be persuaded by reason, but they are moved to act and buy from emotion.

*   <u>People decide on emotion and justify later with logic.</u> With emotions being at the core of our being ("emotionally centered"), logic plays a secondary role in the decision making process to buy ("logically dispersed").

    Logic is dispersed and can be random as it serves the purpose of supporting the emotional decision to buy.

    Logic is inextricably tied to the decision-making process. But logical thought is not the driving power that moves us to decide.

    Emotions are the driving force in what moves people to buy.

*   <u>Scientific evidence supports the position that people are emotionally centered and logically dispersed in their thinking.</u>

    1. Studies on individuals with damage to specific areas of the brain that trig-

ger emotional responses have revealed that IQs are unaffected by such damage. It is the ability to make decisions that suffers.

2. Emotions stimulate the mind thousands of times faster than rational thought does.

3. The left and right hemispheres of the brain have distinctly different functions and abilities:

   * The left brain is quantitative, factual, literal, analytical, and detail-oriented in its processes.

   * The right brain is qualitative, relational, and conceptual, full of imagery, humor, relevance, emotions, and is the seat of our decision-making urges.

* Sales is a contact sport. Appeal to the left brain and connect with the right brain in order to become a better sales professional and realize greater sales success.

   1. Selling is never an emotionally neutral event. Emotions are involved in every business transaction that takes place. The only question that remains is if the emotional experience that the customer has is a positive one or a negative one. If the sales professional makes

the right contact, it will be a positive customer experience emotionally.

2. Facts are left-brain stimulants. Emotions are right-brain stimulants. Bridge the two to gain sales success. This is where most salespeople fail.

3. Do not be a left-brain-only salesperson. Be in your "right mind" and uncover the emotional reasons or criteria for why someone wants to buy. This is what will stimulate the urge for customers to buy.

COGNITIVE CONSCIOUSNESS

Left-Brain Processes

**Emotionally
Centered**

Right-Brain Processes

LOGICALLY DISPERSED

"Other research has shown that in the first few milliseconds of our perceiving something we not only unconsciously comprehend what it is, but decide whether we like it or, not; the cognitive conscious presents our awareness with not just the identity of what we see, but an opinion about it."

DANIEL GOLEMAN

EMOTIONAL INTELLIGENCE[1]

The Lodestar Concept of
Customer Connection

People are Judgmental

CHAPTER THREE
People Are Judgmental

People form opinions of you within seconds of meeting. It has been discovered that a person forms eleven opinions within seven seconds of first meeting someone. Opinions such as educational level, economic level, credibility, believability, trustworthiness, and political and religious background are mentally and emotionally gauged when we first meet an individual. People are judgmental; they are always comparing, always assessing the other person and forming immediate impressions about them.

When my wife, Maureen, and I were first married, we decided that we were going to purchase a new couch and chair for our living room. At the time, we were living in a small split-level home in a neighborhood we loved. I was doing well with my own business, selling financial services and insurance products, and we had managed to save some money to replace the old furniture that we were given.

On the day we actually went looking for a couch and chair, I had just finished working in the yard. We were in a bit of a hurry, so I washed up and quickly changed into a clean pair of jeans, tennis shoes, and a white T-shirt.

The store we decided to go to was an anchor franchise in our local mall. If I said the name, you would recognize it immediately. When we entered the furniture department, we noticed three salespeople a short distance away who were talking amongst themselves. They were aware that we were there, because I saw one of them look right at us when we walked in. They continued their conversation even though customers had just entered into the store area. While they talked, Maureen and I began to look around at what they had to offer.

After about twenty minutes had passed, we came upon the perfect couch and chair combination for our living room. Maureen was so excited. She had finally found a match for her wallpaper and carpet. But still, no salesperson approached us or even asked how we were doing.

So, we made it ever so obvious that we were interested in buying the couch and chair. We sent out all the signals to let them see that we were interested customers: We sat on the couch and chair. We stood around it. We talked about how it might look with our other furniture. We basically did everything possible short of jumping jacks in order to draw a salesperson's attention to us. Finally, I just walked over to them and asked for help.

Total elapsed time from store entry to finally having to ask for help: forty minutes. I was incensed, but I held my tongue for Maureen's sake because she really wanted that couch and chair.

Well, as the story goes, we bought them both and scheduled to have them delivered shortly thereafter. It was not until the sale had been closed and the paperwork signed that the salesperson asked, "Is there anything else I can do for you?"

I couldn't resist. I just had to say something. I replied, "Yes there is something you can do for me, as a matter of fact. The next time I am ever in your store, I would appreciate it if it wouldn't take so long to get someone to help me. For a moment there, I thought no one was ever going to help us out."

Then it happened. I could not believe my ears! The next thing I heard was the salesperson's biased, judgmental attitude betrayed in their response to me.

"I'm sorry," he said. "We just didn't think—" and he stopped himself right there.

"You just didn't think what?" I demanded.

He just stood there guiltily after nearly confessing his prejudice toward me. He didn't have to finish his sentence. I knew exactly what he was going to say, and he knew I knew. He just didn't think we were going to buy anything! That is what he was going to say.

Why? Because in his mind, and in the minds of his other two colleagues, Maureen and I didn't look like a couple who could afford a nice couch and chair. So why bother helping us look for something.

You see, I was dressed in tennis shoes, jeans, and a white T-shirt as mentioned before. My clothes were all very clean and very new-looking. But, nonetheless, he and his colleagues made an immediate assessment of us upon our entering the store-and it wasn't a favorable one.

People are judgmental.

"There are four ways, and only four ways, in which we have contact with the world. We are evaluated and classified by these four contacts: what we do, how we look, what we say, and how we say it."

DALE CARNEGIE

There are three things that most sales professionals can do right away in order to increase their sales and to assure a favorable first impression is made with a customer: give a firm handshake, display a bright smile, and make solid eye contact.

You may be thinking: "This is ridiculous. I need something more concrete, more substantive to help me increase my sales and to go to the next level." But this is some of the best advice I can give you.

The Handshake

In the American culture, we shake hands when meeting someone new, particularly when it comes to business settings. It is an expected custom and practice. So, do it right if that is the case.

Don't give a weak handshake or a limp, "dead fish" handshake. Make it firm, but not crushing. Be brief. Get a good grip. Grab as much hand as you can; let the other person sense your confidence, your strength, and your initiative. Remember, people are judgmental and they are passing judgment on you, beginning with the physical act of the handshake.

A handshake is a connection—not only a physical connection but an emotional one as well. No matter how brief a handshake is or how businesslike it is as a custom, how it is delivered can make the other party either glad to meet you or uncertain about who you are and what you can do for them.

Therefore, when you meet a customer, male or female, make certain you grip their hand firmly and confidently. Avoid the error of shaking someone's hand loosely--without getting a full grasp of their hand. Also, do not treat women any differently when shaking hands.

You see, a handshake is not only a custom in our culture; it is a touchstone that we use to measure the quality of an individual. A weak handshake smacks of a weak character. A weak handshake fails to engender confidence in the person you are meeting. It isn't alluring or endearing at all. In fact, a weak handshake is a turnoff!

Perception Is Reality

A weak handshake does not mean that you are a weak individual. But then, that is irrelevant. The simple fact is perception is reality.

Consider this question: Did the fact that I wore tennis shoes, blue jeans, and a T-shirt into the furniture store necessarily mean that I could not afford a brand-new couch and chair?

No. But it did not change matters for me or my wife, either. We were still treated poorly and had to wait an extraordinary amount of time before being helped. Why? It is because of the tendency of human beings to be judgmental—right or wrong has nothing to do with it.

The customer's perception is all that matters. And, in sales, as in all things, perception is reality. Perception may be inaccurate and may even be a flat-out lie. But, again, that is irrelevant when dealing with beings that are emotionally centered and logically dispersed in how they think, decide, and make judgment calls on things and people.

"I can feel the twinkle in his eyes in his handshake."

HELEN KELLER
COMMENT AFTER MEETING MARK TWAIN

The Eyes

The eyes have been referred to as the windows to the soul. Simply put, the eyes speak of the inner person—their emotions, feelings, and even intelligence. Now, again, perception is reality. Much in the same way the handshake is an emotional connection along the tangible and physical realm, a look of the eyes is an emotional connection along the metaphysical realm.

Eye connection is perhaps the most powerful emotional connection that can be made with another person, and it is the number-one skill to develop, since it has the greatest impact in one-on-one communications.[2]

"An eye can threaten like a loaded and level gun, or it can insult like hissing or kicking; or, in its altered mood, by beams of kindness, it can make the heart dance for joy."

RALPH WALDO EMERSON[3]

Look people in the eye! Research confirms that when a person likes and finds another person interesting or appealing they look at them about 60% to 70% of the time.[4] So let people know you are interested in them. Let them know they are important and have your full attention and care. Make sure that contact is made and held. Grab their hand firmly, stand squarely, look them in the eye, and tell them you are glad to see them.

I am not advocating that you stare your customers down. Sales is a contact sport. Connect with the eyes, but make it brief. Let them know you notice and acknowledge them as well—on a personal and professional level. Failure to make eye contact will build suspicion and other negative feelings within the mind of the customer.

If the individual looks away, that's okay. Each person has their own threshold of comfort when it comes to making eye contact. Some cultures even frown on strong eye contact under certain circumstances. But as a general rule, briefly look away every five to six seconds. Let them, and you, decompress a little so that there is no perceived pressure or discomfort in meeting you.

In the American business culture, we shake hands firmly and we look people in the eye when we greet and speak with them. If we do anything less, we communicate weakness, lack of confidence, uncertainty, and even deception upon our part.

Perception is reality.

"When the eyes say one thing and the tongue another, a practiced man relies on the language of the first."

RALPH WALDO EMERSON

The Smile

Another powerful habit to develop is the habit of smiling often and deliberately. A smile is disarming. It draws people near and dispels their fears. It makes you approachable...safe. It invites conversation and "greases" the process of the sales conversation. What I am not advocating is a false, forced smile that looks false and forced! I am talking about a natural, relaxed, genuine expression that attracts people toward you rather than pushing them away from you.

Charles Schwab once told Dale Carnegie that his smile had been "worth a million dollars"...literally![5] It is the best and most direct way of saying, "I like you. I'm happy and comfortable in your presence." It is a connection on a social and emotional level that puts you in a favorable light with anyone in an instant. A smile differentiates you from all the other so-called "sales professionals" out there. Do not minimize its power in making a client and loyal friend out of someone.

Often when I speak to sales professionals about smiling, they look at me with a confused expression. That is because the great majority of salespeople *think* they smile enough. If you share the same thinking, put it to the test. Next time you are in a buying situation or observing a sales professional with a potential client, note their behavior. Compare their behavior to other sales professionals you have observed and see how often and at what times they smile. You will discover that most salespeople need to work at smiling more often during their sales conversations with customers.

"A man without a smiling face must not open a shop."

CHINESE PROVERB

Here is a quick test of your smiling skills: Do friends, family members or even coworkers occasionally ask you if everything is alright or if there is something wrong when, in actuality, everything is fine with you? If this happens to you, then you are sending them a visual message that doesn't project a favorable perception in other people's eyes.

Smile. Exaggerate it if you have a facial expression that is naturally stern and serious. If you have to, get a mirror and smile in front of it. Critique yourself. Or ask a trusted friend to render their honest opinion of what your face is "saying." I know it can be a difficult task to be open to such critical assessments of this nature, but it is necessary or else you will remain the curmudgeon that others perceive you to be—and perception is reality.

People are judgmental. Make the *best* of their first impressions of you. Start with a firm, confident handshake, look them in the eye, and give them a "million-dollar smile." In the end, you will gain a customer and win a friend.

CHAPTER THREE: KEY NOTES

People Are Judgmental

* It is a fact of life that people form immediate opinions of other people within seconds of meeting them.

* Perception is reality. Perception is the only reality that matters to the customer.

* Perception can be inaccurate. This is irrelevant to the customer. Accuracy is not a measure of customer reality. Perception is the only measure of customer reality.

* The sales professional must understand the power of first impressions and try to gain as favorable an opinion in the eyes of the customer as possible.

* There are three things that most sales professionals can do to gain a favorable customer opinion (judgment):

    1. Deliver a good handshake.
        * Grab as much hand as you can, and be firm about it!
        * Do not differentiate between male and female handshaking.
        * Be sensitive to special situations (e.g., arthritis, etc.).

2. Look people in the eye.
    * Make brief and regular contact.
    * Don't stare.
    * Be sensitive to their comfort level in looking at you.

3. Smile.
    * Smile naturally, often, and when appropriate.
    * Smiles draw people to you and help you to open up a conversation.
    * Smiles dispel the fear of being forced into buying something.
    * A smile helps break down a person's natural resistance to the sales process.

"Can I help you?"

"No, thanks. I'm just looking."

The Lodestar Concept of

Customer Connection

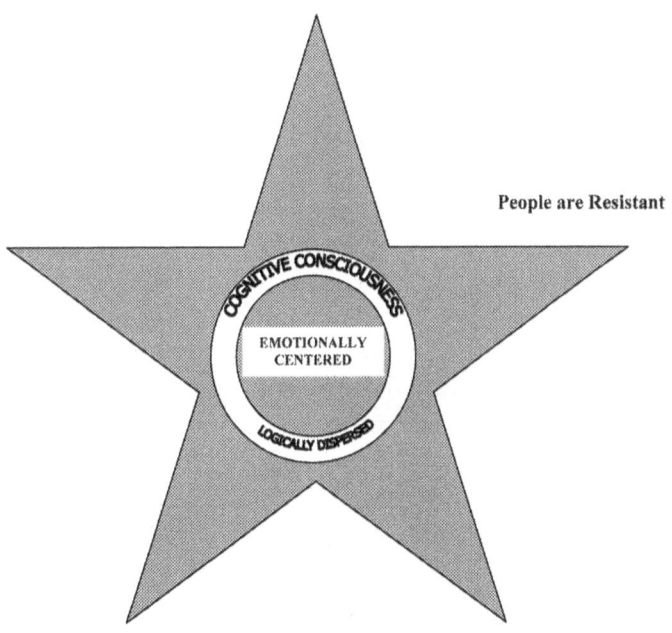

People are Resistant

CHAPTER FOUR

People Are Naturally Resistant

It is true. As social beings possessing engaging minds and spirits, we oftentimes have a natural tendency to be resistant. We are resistant to change, differences in routine, and new ways of thinking. We are resistant to all kinds of things that we are not used to or familiar with, particularly those things related to the buying process.

When buying or simply transacting business that involves the exchange of money, customers automatically put up the "caution" sign and begin to push back, if not totally retreat, from the sales and buying cycle.

Consider your own reactions, for example, when in a department store you are approached by a salesperson. First of all, what is the most common question you are asked when initially approached? "May I help you?" This question serves up the nearly involuntary response of, "No, thanks. I'm just looking."

So is it really true that you are not interested in receiving help? As a customer, is all you are interested in doing is looking at merchandise and not wanting to buy? Of course not, people go to stores and malls not to just look, but to buy. I will agree that they are looking at things--but they are looking at things to eventually buy someday. They may not be looking to buy that moment or that day. But when people look, they look to eventually get! It is that simple.

So, then, why exactly do people resist assistance when shopping? Why don't they just come out and make it clear what they are doing and intending? It is because customers need space. They need distance, a kind of mental and emotional cushion whenever the unfamiliar, uncomfortable, or unpredictable arises. Resistance is a safety mechanism that is triggered within every person whenever a situation is uncertain.

Earlier, we discovered that people are judgmental; they make split-second assessments of environment, situations, and people. In the dynamics of making snap judgments, people seek distance and ease from these uncertain situations.

It is like the lioness that is patient and calculated in stalking her prey. First, she circles, observing the nature and character of the hunted. Then, she assesses the environment and only makes her move when she is comfortable with the notion she will overcome and succeed in her efforts. She never moves in quickly or rashly. She keeps her distance; comfortable knowing that she can strike when she feels the time is right or run if danger ensues.

> *"When you feel someone is trying to get you to do what they want you to do, the relationship, by definition, becomes adversarial and by reflex you try to protect yourself. That's where resistance, suspicion and hostility come from. Traditional selling, regardless of how cloaked, is hunter versus prey."*
>
> JACQUES WERTH AND NICHOLAS E. RUBEN
> *HIGH PROBABILITY SELLING*[1]

Do Not Internalize Customer Resistance

I am not implying that all sales situations involve a hunt-or-be-hunted relationship. But, unfortunately, many do resemble this traditional sales methodology, which contributes to one of the major causes of sales resistance itself. Yet, even in the midst of the most non-threatening sales environment, customers innately operate on a protracted and calculated level. Whether that behavior is logical or illogical is irrelevant; it is simply a fact of human nature. We all are resistant to the buying process.

So why is natural resistance by the customer so important to understand? First, understanding human beings and their natural tendency to resist the sales process will help you to have the right perspective mentally.

Why is it that the majority of sales professionals entering the profession commonly leave within a short time of starting their careers? And why is it that sales managers and sales recruiters are always so eager, and often desperate, to find and hire people into one of the greatest professions in the world? It is because of burnout.

Salespeople are particularly vulnerable to discouragement, emotional stress, and pressure created from a misunderstanding about natural customer resistance. Some salespeople burn out quietly, and others go out with a bright flash and a loud boom! They simply are not able to weather the emotional strains that customer resistance creates.

Sales professionals often internalize customer resistance--that is they often turn the customer's natural inclination to resist the sales process into feelings of frustration, doubt, and depression over not having closed the sale. They make resistance a personal matter for them rather than a natural step in the sales process itself. That is a huge mistake.

People resist the salesperson and the sales process because, in their nature, they must. Rarely is resistance a personal matter between you, the salesperson, and the customer. Often, it is simply a natural case of behaving as humans will—and that is to be resistant at first. Don't make it more than it is, and don't take pushback or skepticism—or whatever other form resistance may take--personally. That would be a tragic mistake, especially if you plan to be a career sales professional and to be happy.

Plan Ahead to Deal with Customer Resistance

Second, understanding human beings and their natural tendency to resist the sales process will help your efforts to be successful. As has been said many times before, your will to win and be successful in sales is not as important as your will to plan to win. Plenty of sales professionals are determined to succeed, yet the majority of them end up failing. Why? Well, if it isn't burnout that causes them to fail, it is the breakdown in *planning* to succeed that causes failure. Mark it down: One of the core traits of successful sales professionals is their determination in planning to win.

Consider again how people are judgmental, and link it to the fact that people are also resistant to the sales process. These two tenets of human nature ought to be enough supporting evidence for the sales professional's need to plan ahead and develop an effective first-impression strategy, which would include a process designed to melt customer resistance.

The first impression is vital to a powerful close and overcoming customer resistance. So make sure when you greet customers you greet them with a firm handshake, a friendly smile, bright eyes, and with the same deference that you demand when you yourself are a customer. The golden rule: Make customers feel good and feel special from the start and their resistance toward you and the sales process will melt away.

Finally, understanding the customer's natural tendency to resist will help underpin your resolve to serve their needs and reach your own personal goals. Resistance, as a part of the sales process, provides us with the forum to connect emotionally with people. Without labors under the heat of a noonday sun, there would not be the satisfaction of a cold, clear glass of water. The fact that people are judgmental and resistant sets the stage for emotional connection and relationship-building with other people—and that is not a bad thing

If customer resistance is ever to be taken "personally," it should only be so in the form of a personal challenge in overcoming it and meeting your own personal sales goals.

Several years ago, my wife and I decided to recarpet a couple of rooms in our house. So, we jumped into the car and went to the carpet store. As soon as we walked into the store, we were spotted by the salesperson. So I did what every red-blooded man would do: I shoved my wife in the direction of the salesperson as a decoy while I walked in the opposite direction (my version of resistance).

The salesperson approached my wife and, as I watched from a distance, I noticed several remarkable things about this individual's style.

First of all, she didn't say, "Can I help you?" Thank goodness! Instead, she walked up to my wife with a pleasant and natural smile, looked her in the eye, shook her hand, and said, "Hi, I'm Mary."

What transpired in the next several minutes can only be described as a beautiful thing. She didn't talk about "this carpet" on sale or "that carpet" on discount. Instead, she began to ask my wife questions, questions about who we were, what we were hoping to accomplish, if we were considering a particular color scheme or theme for a room, and so on. Bottom line: She was breaking down any natural barriers of resistance we had by getting into our world and talking about us and not herself or the carpet they had to sell.

As I listened to more of her conversation with my wife, I began to think to myself," She's a pretty nice person." So I moved closer and soon found myself joining the conversation and enjoying the experience of being there. The first five to ten minutes of the discussion centered on "us" and what we liked and wanted to do with our house.

Product and price did not enter the conversation until later. It wasn't until sufficient time was spent in talking about what mattered to us did the salesperson begin to mention anything about cost or what they had available in the store.

I would like to tell you that we bought carpet from her that same day, but we didn't. What we did do was decide that we were going to buy from her, though. We just were not ready right then based on our own timing and personal finances. But, nonetheless, we eventually did buy from her. Why? Because we liked her. We connected with her and formed a favorable opinion (judgment) of her. She allowed us some space and didn't smother us with facts and figures right away. She didn't display an aggressive sales style. Instead, she was relaxed, friendly, had a nice smile, firm handshake, and showed interest in us—in *us*!

Undeterred by my obvious display of buyer's resistance, she melted away our natural resistance and won two customers for life. From that day on, she was to be our "carpet lady."

CHAPTER FOUR: KEY NOTES

People Are Resistant

* <u>People are resistant to change,</u> differences, new things, and the unfamiliar.

* <u>Consider your own reactions when buying</u>.

> "Can I help you?" "No thanks. I'm just looking": The most common customer response that betrays our natural tendency to resist the sales process.

* <u>Understanding natural resistance to the sales process helps sales professionals to</u>

    1. stay in the business for the long term.
       * People resist because it is in their nature to resist. Take resistance personally only to the extent that it is the framework from which the sales professional can begin to build a personal relationship with the customer.
       * Don't internalize customer resistance. It is not you they are resistant about...it is the process of buying and selling that customers resist.

2. prepare to be successful.
    *   A common trait among successful sales professionals is their habit of planning ahead for things, such as, planning ahead to make a good first impression with customers, planning ahead to overcome resistance, and planning ahead to make the customer feel special and enjoy the buying experience. Your will to win is not as important as your will to plan to win!

3. never give up on the sales process.
    *   Resistance will come. Accept it. Work with it. Don't let it be the excuse for not being successful or building meaningful customer relationships.

"People are not interested in you. They are not interested in me. They are interested in themselves—morning, noon, and after dinner."

DALE CARNEGIE
HOW TO WIN FRIENDS AND INFLUENCE PEOPLE[1]

The Lodestar Concept of

Customer Connection

People Are Egocentric

CHAPTER FIVE
People Are Egocentric

A wise person once told me that the best and quickest way to endear people to you is to allow them to talk about what they like to talk about. Over the years, that has proved to be good advice for me.

Why is that? The explanation first lies in our egocentric natures and perspectives. Like the toddler that is often mused at for thinking the world revolves around them, adults seemingly never grow out of that same me-oriented stage. Yes, we do grow and mature, becoming conscious of "another" world and "other" perspectives and needs than our own. But the basic egocentric view of the world remains every bit a part of our nature as it was when we were children.

It is impossible for us to live and think otherwise. Our eyes, ears, and skin are sensory probes that connect at one central location: the mind, which interprets life around us from a single egocentric perspective. Thus, we naturally develop over time an egocentric perspective on all matters of life.

The question of whether or not our egocentric nature is a bad thing is not in debate here. It is merely a fact of life that is to be recognized and understood particularly as it relates to our discussion of sales as a contact sport.

Since we know how people are in respect to their world view and orientation (egocentric), why not leverage this knowledge in the sales process? That is to say, if "me" and "I" are the alpha pronouns of our world view and how we perceive and communicate, then why not allow customers to talk about what they want to talk about? Invariably, that boils down to one common subject: the subject of "me," everyone's favorite topic of discussion.

"Mr. Charming"

Not long ago, my wife and I went into a car dealership looking to buy a new vehicle. Our fourteen-year-old van had over two hundred thousand miles on it, and we were ready for something new. The dealership we chose was a longstanding local business with name recognition in the community and a large selection of vehicles to choose from. It was a good place to start.

When we walked into the showroom, all of our protective sales-resistance measures were fully deployed. In other words, I was psychologically prepared to be cautious and maintain distance with any salesperson that would approach us.

Within seconds upon entering, a tall man of about thirty years of age walked up to us. He was neatly dressed and had impeccably groomed hair. I was instantly postured psychologically to make things go at my pace and not too quickly.

I observed how he looked, his demeanor, and noticed his mannerisms and how he addressed us when he introduced himself. Although he had a firm and confident handshake, I noticed how he failed to look directly at me, favoring my wife instead when it came to who he kept his attention on. Now I can understand why he would favor my wife over me, but it soon became obvious and uncomfortable for her as the conversation progressed.

Also, he had what I would characterize as an insincere smile—what might be called a smirk—when he first greeted us. It wasn't a full and genuine "glad to meet you" greeting. It was more like a smile that was hiding some secret joke that only he knew. He was having a laugh at our expense. At least it appeared that way, and the customer's perception is reality...the only reality that matters.

Another fatal flaw I noted in our encounter with this salesperson was his need to do all the talking. After his smirk and "Hi, I'm Bob" routine, he went right into a speech about how they were the biggest and best dealership in the entire area and how they had a larger selection of cars and vans than anyone else.

Big deal, I thought. So what does that mean to me? Then he rolled right into telling us about their rebates and financing programs, what models were selling at a discount, and which auto manufacturers they specialized in.

He didn't seem to care about us at all. Never asking us questions about what we were interested in, or what we were thinking or wanting to do in regard to buying a new vehicle. No, instead he was operating on his own agenda, talking about cars, vans, and prices without any concern for what was important to us. He failed to get into our world even though we would have gladly let him in...all he had to do was ask, that is, ask us questions about what we wanted.

He even was guilty of allowing his eyes to drift away and fix momentarily on something behind us while in the middle of our conversation. He wasn't even paying attention to us!

Instead of getting us to talk and open up in order to break our natural resistance and gain a favorable judgment position, he chose the most common route sales professionals take: talking about what they want to talk about rather than what the customer wants to talk about.

This gentleman was from the school of sales that says, "Selling is something you do *to* someone." I propose that he would have been better to consider the opposite sales philosophy: "Selling is something we do *for* someone."

I didn't like him and neither did my wife. I knew almost immediately after meeting him that we were not going to buy from him. I'm certain that from his point of view, he viewed himself as a model producer—a well-spoken, smartly dressed, handsome sales expert that couldn't be resisted. But, to us, he was perceived as a silver-tongued hustler pushing empty promises and smiling only to get what he wanted. Of the two impressions, the only one that mattered was ours. So we left, never to return.

The Younger Salesman

In contrast, we visited a dealership a few miles away, one that was a bit smaller and lesser-known than the first one we went to. To say our experience there was much different—and better—is an understatement.

When we entered the showroom, we were quickly greeted by a salesman just as before. But one of the remarkable differences from our previous experience was that this salesman was genuinely friendly. He had a warm and natural smile, with direct and balanced eye contact between the two of us.

He was well-groomed, professionally dressed, and had a relaxed demeanor about him. I guessed him to be around twenty-two to twenty-three years of age, considerably younger than my wife and me.

He immediately began to talk about football and the Ohio State Buckeyes. It wasn't that he was a psychic and perceived in some mystical way that I was a fan of the team. He simply was observant. It was a chilly day in Ohio, and I happened to be wearing an OSU football pullover jacket.

Also, he was very conscious not to exclude my wife from the conversation. He asked her if she watched football or was a fan of the Ohio State Buckeyes and then rolled into some open-ended questions about our family, where we lived, and where we had originally grown up.

He was a friendly, pleasant person, very interested in what we had to say, quite a refreshing difference from our previous experience with Mr. Charming. For a change, we got to talk about what *we* were interested in.

"You can pick out actors by the glazed look that comes into their eyes when the conversation wanders away from themselves."

MICHAEL WILDING

Mr. Charming wasn't real or genuine. If he was not dominating the discussion on his terms and talking about what he wanted to talk about, he was not satisfied. But that is not what my wife and I wanted. We wanted our needs, our concerns, and our wants to be satisfied.

The same goes for you when you are in the buying process. Sales professionals who appreciate this fact learn to tailor and shape their language, their approaches, and their demeanor toward what is important to the customer and not to what is important to them.

The younger salesman was wise. He established more than just gaining rapport with us, even though he did manage to connect with us quite naturally in that regard. What he accomplished went far beyond the simple definition of friendliness and good conversation in opening the sales conversation.

First of all, he created a favorable first impression with us. That's right. When we walked into the car showroom, he greeted us warmly with a genuine smile and a firm, but not crushing, handshake. He looked each of us in the eyes and was careful to make sure he maintained balanced contact.

His overall appearance was neat, professional-looking, and not overdone. And, so, within seconds of meeting him, we had decided that he was the kind of person we could buy from, the kind that was not threatening and who seemed to care about what we wanted and needed.

The conversation never went to cars until after adequate discussion and explanation about what we wanted to talk about was established. Remember, people are judgmental. We passed judgment on him, and he got a favorable first-impression grade from us.

Secondly, he quickly sensed what might be interesting for my wife and me to talk about. Now, for me, it was clearly football and all kinds of sports. For my wife, he explored the subject of sports but quickly sensed the subject of family, home, and community were good subjects to open with and make a connection with her on. He was a smart sales professional who simply allowed us to talk about what we like to talk about.

Here is what happens when you allow the sales conversation to be steered by the customer:

1. It helps you to gain a favorable first impression, and it gets people to like you. (People are judgmental.)

2. It takes the pressure off the customer. It relaxes them and keeps them in a realm they are comfortable in—the familiar—and breaks down a customer's natural tendency to resist. (People are resistant.)

3. It takes the pressure off the sales expert by allowing the customer to talk about what they want to talk about.

4. It is the first step toward building a relationship and establishing value (which we will address later in the book) in the mind of the customer.

5. It suggests that you are "like" them. Talk about what interests the customer, and it sends a subtle and powerful message that you are not much different than they are. That is comforting and reassuring to the customer and says that you understand them.

6. It suggests you are interested in them enough to listen. People have a sense that they are never fully listened to in life. Listening shows interest, deference to their ideas and opinions, and respect for them as unique, special individuals.

7. It is a good way to uncover relevant facts, needs, and wants that you can assist in fulfilling. Often, the emotional criterion for why someone would buy is revealed when the customer is allowed to talk about what they want to talk about.

8. It fosters openness and builds momentum for the sales interview to continue.

9. Finally, it is considerate and kind to give the customer what they want...an opportunity to be heard and understood. That is a gift they will come back for time-after-time-after-time.

People are egocentric. They are dominated by the phenomenon of the self-centered mindset, where 15% of the brain's functions are focused on understanding and processing language, and the other 85% is busied with thoughts of self-interest, personal problems, dreams, and self-gratification.[2] Sales professionals that understand this part of our psychological makeup can naturally and easily frame their questions and responses so that the customer perceives that their interests are being considered and served.

CHAPTER FIVE: KEY NOTES

People Are Egocentric

"Few are agreeable in conversation, because each thinks of what he intends to say than of what others are saying, and listens no more when he himself has a chance to speak."

FRANÇOIS DE LA ROCHEFOUCAULD

"I often quote myself. It adds spice to my conversation."

GEORGE BERNARD SHAW

---

*   <u>People have a naturally developed egocentric view of the world</u> that is first observed in childhood and carried into adulthood. Their interests and perspectives are at the core of all their thinking and responses in life. Thus, the very topics of interest the salesperson must focus on are those that the customer thinks about most, interests that are important to them, and things they like to talk about.

*   <u>Understanding this tendency toward self-interest in connection to conversations helps sales professionals to</u>

1. formulate positive first-impression conversation strategies that focus on what the customer wants to talk about. Be observant, sensitive, and intuitive about interests and likes of the customer.

     * Specific, open-ended questions designed to draw out customer interests need to be formulated in advance and used when building customer rapport.

2. relax and gain confidence in the sales conversation.

3. build relationships. People never feel that they are listened to fully in life, especially by sales professionals. So give them what they want!

4. be liked, erode customer resistance, and gain momentum toward moving deeper into the sales conversation.

5. give the customer what they want: a chance to talk about something they like, understand, appreciate, and don't have to think long and hard about.

"Pretend that every single person you meet has a sign around his or her neck that says, Make me feel important. Not only will you succeed in sales, you will succeed in life."

MARY KAY ASH
FOUNDER OF MARY KAY COSMETICS

The Lodestar Concept of Customer Connection

People Are Individualistic

CHAPTER SIX
People Are Individualistic

"People have an innate need to be valued and to know that they count for something."

RON WILLINGHAM
THE PEOPLE PRINCIPLE[1]

Each of us is individualistic by nature, possessing an innate longing to feel special, appreciated, unique, and valued among people and by people. It is what educator and philosopher Dr. John Dewey called one of the deepest urges a human being can have: "the desire to feel important." Freud termed it "the desire to be great." And American philosopher and physician William James said that it was "the deepest principle in human nature; the craving to be appreciated."[2]

We are naturally drawn to people that feed this private hunger, this craving to be special, important, "great!" It has been called the Basic Binary Code of Behavioral Choice, which involves "moving toward what makes us feel good and what we like and moving away from what makes us feel bad and what we dislike."[3] It is this very desire, or binary code, of ours that has spawned industries whose primary goal is the satisfaction of individualistic desires and cravings to feel important.

"If I can point to one common trait that all master salespeople and corporate leaders seem to have in common, it is this: Great salespeople have a brilliant ability to make every valuable or potentially valuable person they meet feel like the most important person in the world."

DAVID P. SNYDER
HOW TO MIND-READ YOUR CUSTOMERS[4]

The greeting-card industry, for example, thrives upon our basic human need to be validated, to feel special and valued. Valentine's Day, weddings, anniversaries, and birthdays, to name a few, are occasions capitalized upon by scores of card manufacturers in a marketing effort to gain customer dollars out of these individualistic cravings. Thousands of different cards are designed for one purpose and one purpose only: to make the recipient feel special. Why? Because "special" sells and special appeals to people! Remember, it is a craving.

The fast-growing day-spa industry is another example of growth built upon the basic human desire to feel special and valued. Promises of pampering, relaxation, and attention are showered upon customers that "deserve" a special getaway for themselves or that special someone in their lives.

The cruise industry, which has long advanced the notion of specialized attention for its passengers, has become increasingly aware of the competitive edge crew-to-passenger ratios can give them over the competition. Today, you can find cruise lines that advertise two to three crew members to every one passenger as a means of attracting seafarers toward specialized, unfettered sailing pleasure. The buying public is craving this special attention and booking it a year in advance in many cases.

What does all of this mean for the sales professional? Well, it means that the sales professional who knows how to make people feel special and valued wins. Yet, many of my peers are guilty of depriving clients, and potential clients as well, of this very basic need. They miss the opportunity to make a friend, a fan, and a customer for life by failing to get people to feel special and uniquely individualistic.

What, then, can be done to avoid this situation and to give the customer what they want? Well, if we consider and honor four simple rules when dealing with customers, we will always satisfy their craving to feel special and important.

Rule #1: Acknowledgement

If there is one violation of the sales process that is a "game breaker," it is the failure of sales professionals to acknowledge customers and greet them warmly when they first see them.

"One of the biggest complaints customers make is that they are ignored, that nobody pays any attention to them. Even before any transaction begins, the customer is already feeling bad. By keeping an eye open for customers coming into your domain, you can take the initiative to greet, welcome, acknowledge or put them at ease as appropriate. Even if you are dealing with another customer, it is not difficult to gesture to a new customer that you will come to them in a moment or two. Such small gestures add a high degree of emotional value."

DAVID FREEMANTLE
WHAT CUSTOMERS LIKE ABOUT YOU[5]

Violate the Rule of Acknowledgment, and you might as well forget about the other three rules because the customer will shut you off and abandon you as quickly as they sense they are being ignored.

Not long ago I went to see an attorney about some trust work. The client reception area was nicely decorated with hardwood furniture, beautiful thick Berber carpet, and very expensive artwork tastefully framed on the walls.

Across the room was the receptionist counter. Sitting there with a phone to her ear, intently listening to someone on the other end was a woman who was there to greet and register walk-in appointments. So, naturally, I walked up to the counter and stood there patiently waiting to be acknowledged, signaled to sign in, or whatever.

The problem was, I stood there, and I stood there, and I stood there, waiting as patiently and politely as possible with no indication from the woman that she was going to give me what I wanted. All at once, my blood pressure began to slowly rise and my opinion of the receptionist—and the attorney who I had yet to meet—was quickly falling.

She was ignoring me, plain and simple. At least, that was my perception of the situation and, again, perception is reality. I was not feeling special at all.

Some of you may be thinking, "But she was busy on the phone with someone, probably another client of theirs. Perhaps she was embroiled in a complaint call or some problem situation." This is absolutely possible, but it doesn't change the circumstances or my perception of the receptionist or the attorney she represented.

And although she was busy at the moment, that didn't relieve her of the responsibility to acknowledge me and make me feel welcome and valued, someone to be counted.

Not once did she look up from her desk. The phone was clasped to her ear, her head was bent, and her eyes looked down. She was in a world that didn't include me as one of its members. I felt awkward, and I also knew that she knew I was standing there waiting.

Do I turn and sit down? I thought. Should I sign in? Should I cough to get her to acknowledge me? What do I do?

What I did do was eventually walk out. Oh, I did turn and sit down at first, thinking I'd give her the benefit of the doubt. But when ten minutes had passed and she was still on the phone, still not acknowledging my presence, I left never to return—and the business I intended on doing there went right out the door with me to be given to another attorney.

It is obvious what she did was wrong. If she had simply looked me in the eye and acknowledged me—through a smile, nod, or other gesture—it wouldn't have been so bad. In this case, I could see that she was busy. I was willing to wait an acceptable amount of time before being acknowledged.

But what I wasn't going to tolerate, and what most customers will not tolerate, is being ignored—left standing, feeling awkward and unappreciated. Don't be guilty of violating this cardinal rule of salesmanship: the Rule of Acknowledgment.

Rule #2: Attention

Attention is one of those things each of us simply can't get enough of in our lives. When transacting business, it is *imperative* that the sales professional give the customer their undivided attention.

What does undivided attention really mean? According to author and sales expert Ron Willingham, it has everything to do with breaking "preoccupation" and "tuning the world out and the customer in." It also means investing time with the customer and "being there for them," ever present to meet their needs for that moment.

"There is no mystery to successful business inter-course...exclusive attention to the person who is speaking to you . . ."

CHARLES W. ELIOT, FORMER HARVARD PRESIDENT

Too often, we allow preoccupation and inter-ruptions to intrude upon our contact with cus-tomers, making them feel incidental and unim-portant. A friend of mine told me about a time he was in his insurance agent's office talking about his life insurance program. My friend, having recently suffered a heart attack, was concerned about his family's welfare after his death. The disturbing part of the story amid the obvious prospect of my friend dying was the manner in which the agent treated him...he didn't really give my friend his full, undivided attention on such a grave and serious subject.

I was told that while they discussed my friend's situation and his concerns, the agent's eyes, al-most imperceptibly, wandered off to something out of the window of his office. Apparently, the agent had a large office window almost directly behind where his clients sat. To make things worse, my friend tells me that the agent took two "quick" phone calls, as they were characterized by the agent, while they were meeting about my friend's concerns for his family and their future.

Imagine that—a customer with deep family concerns consulting with his agent, his *advisor*, on matters that will affect his family's future and having to compete for his agent's attention against some unknown subject of interest out the window or a couple of quick calls that could have waited. My friend was disgusted and frustrated with the agent. He was disgusted because of all the money he had already invested with this individual in life, home, auto, and health insurance, and he was frustrated because he knew the agent hadn't given any real thought to his circumstance. Successful business intercourse relies on *exclusive* attention.

Rule #3: Appreciation

"Thank you" and you're welcome" are what I term the lost social courtesies. There are others I can mention, but these two, especially "thank you," are some of the easiest to master yet the most often violated when it comes to making the customer feel special.

As a customer, how many times have you paid for an item—for instance, at a grocery store, gas station, or clothing store—and you don't get a thank you from the salesperson in return? How does that make you feel? Does it make you feel like a valued customer or does it make you feel unappreciated?

Transacting business is always an emotional experience. Sometimes that emotional experience is intense, and other times it is subdued. But in every instance, customers are emotional when business is transacting. Money, or the exchange of value from one person to another, is an emotional trigger for everyone.

This basic need to be appreciated ought to remind every sales professional to thank the customer at every opportunity and in every transaction no matter how minor or routine. To do anything less is to diminish the customer's sense of importance and self-worth.

Failure to show the requisite appreciation for someone's business is the equivalent of saying, "Give me your money...now who is next?" No one likes that kind of treatment or wants to feel that way—no one.

Are you sensitive to your customer's time? Do you make them wait unnecessarily? Do you apologize when they do have to wait longer than usual? Do you acknowledge them when they walk into your place of business? Do you listen closely to what they say...give them your attention? Are you sensitive to their wants and needs? Do you say thank you when they do business with you?

These are all important questions that every sales professional must ask themselves. Any answer other than "yes" has to be corrected or else your client base and future growth opportunities will surely erode.

It is the customer's Basic Binary Code of Behavioral Choice to gravitate toward those things that make them feel good and to shy away and even shun those things that don't. What direction are your customers going in?

Are they drawn to you by way of acknowledgement and attention? Is there a specific "thank you" strategy in your business practice to show your appreciation for the customer and their choice to buy from you?

Do they feel good about their buying experience with you? If not, they will seek out some other sales professional to do business with who will appreciate them and make them feel special. It just won't be you.

Rule #4: Affection

By affection, I mean having a liking toward people, or customers. Do you like people? Do you really care about them and in selling them what they want and need? Our affections, values, and *likes* correlate directly to our behavior and speech. If I like and value someone, then it will show. I will naturally make them a priority, consider their needs over my own, and protect and provide for them.

"Man is what he believes."

ANTON CHEKHOV

People naturally and automatically will stay true to an inner guide, or template, of affection and personal values that they possess when interacting with others. Our actions and reactions to the world around us are, for the most part, consistent with those values and affections we have for people. Yes, we can mask our true feelings at times, possibly even for quite a while. But when we are allowed to be ourselves, so to speak, we naturally behave as we think and feel inside.

That is why I highly recommend, first and foremost, that sales professionals *like* people! It is that simple. Your customers will sense this in you and will be drawn to you because of it. It makes them feel good; it makes them feel special and important. That is something that they don't regularly get in life, particularly when it comes to transacting business.

People are individualistic; they desire to feel special, important, and valued. *Acknowledge* them whenever you see them, give them your *attention*, and let them know you *appreciate* their business and the relationship you have with them. And always have great *affection* for your customers as husbands, wives, daughters, sons, mothers, fathers, sisters, brothers, and as individuals who matter. Follow these four simple rules and you will win customers for life.

"There is one all-important law of human conduct...if obeyed, will bring us countless friends and constant happiness. But the very instant we break the law; we shall get into endless trouble. The law is this: Always make the other person feel important."

DALE CARNEGIE

CHAPTER SIX: KEY NOTES

People Are Individualistic

* People have an innate craving to feel special, important, and valued.

* Consider your own buying experience—positive and negative. What is it that you liked or didn't like about the salesperson or place where you were looking to buy? How much did your feelings play into your ultimate decision to buy? How did the sales expert make you feel?

* The sales professional who knows how to make people feel special and valued wins!

* There are four simple rules to satisfy the customer "craving" to feel important and special:

> Rule #1: Acknowledgment—Never, never, never make the customer feel ignored. All other rules are secondary to this one.

> Rule #2: Attention—Undivided, uninterrupted, exclusive attention is what the customer deserves...and demands.

> Rule #3: Appreciation—"Thank you" is a good verbal gesture to start with.

Always show appreciation for the customer's business, for their loyalty, their patronage, and their investment in you, the sales professional.

Rule #4: Affection—How you feel or think about a customer is automatically mirrored, or made manifest, in your actions and speech. If you "truly" like and respect the customer, customers will truly like and respect you back.

"...Effective communication is a lot more than simply transferring information from me to you, or vice versa. There is a gate between us through which communication must pass...The Gatekeeper has complete power to grant or deny access to our listeners' higher analytical and decision making processes. A New Communicator is a person who knows how to befriend the Gatekeeper."

BERT DECKER

YOU'VE GOT TO BE BELIEVED TO BE HEARD[1]

The Lodestar Concept of
Customer Connection

People Are Visual/Vocal/Verbal

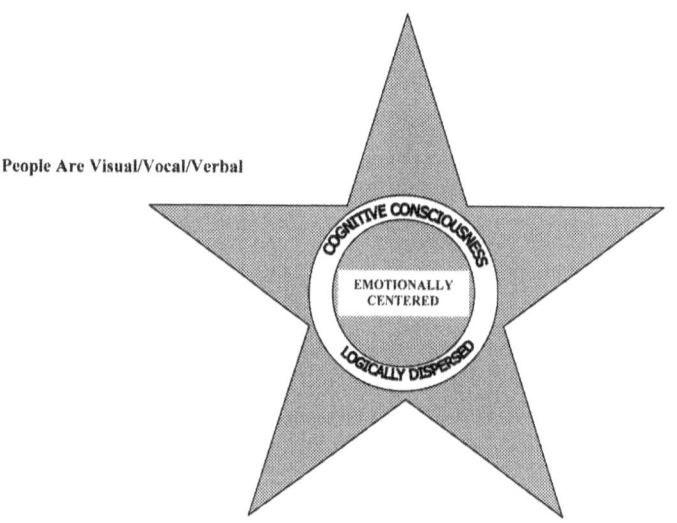

CHAPTER SEVEN
People Connect Visually, Vocally, and Verbally

When I speak to sales professionals, one of the most important discussions I have with them is in regard to understanding the three components of communication—visual, vocal, and verbal—and the impact each has on persuading others.

The fact that I can be seen when communicating to a group or individual is, of course, the visual component or realm. It alone has its own message and measured power to persuade.

My being heard reflects the vocal component of communication, the sounds influenced by the vocal elements of pitch, tone, inflection, cadence, and pauses. Each element possesses its own capabilities to change or direct the meaning of a message and influence its listener.

Finally, the very content within my voice—the words or verbal content—is obviously a part of the message and is the component so often discussed at length by sales experts when it comes to the effectiveness of a sales conversation to influence a customer's thinking.

All three components of communication carry with them an inherent weight or gravity to influence. When successfully used in harmony, they exert a tremendous amount of positive sales energy and strength to change customer thinking and behavior. Bert Decker, nationally recognized communications expert, calls this energy "the impact to persuade and be believed."

Each component has its part in the sales conversation and is inextricably tied to the emotionally centered nature of people. They are what I call, the "emotional connective tissue" that links the message sent by the sales professional to the message received by the customer.

Emotional Connective Tissue

UCLA Professor Albert Mehrabian, in his 1967 landmark study, measured the effect that each communication component had on the believability, or impact, of a message to persuade and change thinking. He found that the impact, or the transmission of a message and its believability, can be quantified in terms of percentages, as indicated below[2]:

Visual Communication	55%
Vocal Communication	38%
Verbal Communication	7%

More recent evidence in human communication asserts that approximately 80% of a "message sent and a message received" is confined to the realm of the nonverbal (e.g., vocal intonations, gestures, posture, facial expressions, eye contact, dress, vocal tempo, and timing). Our literal verbal exchanges pale in comparison to the weight and impact inherent in what we see and how we say things.[3]

Such research suggests that a communication hierarchy exists when seeking to connect emotionally with customers during the sales conversation. That hierarchy begins first and foremost with the visual realm and moves through the vocal and verbal components of communication.

It also suggests that the need to connect, to effectively communicate with power and impact, is rooted at a subconscious emotional level that overrides processes of the conscious rational mind.

To summarize simply: A picture is worth a thousand words. Also, it is not *what* you say that has the greatest impact on the listener; it is *how* you say it that does. Let's examine each component separately.

The Visual Component

The nerve pathways between the eyes and the brain are twenty-five times larger than those of the ears. Our visual ability is the only sense that contains actual brain cells. It has been estimated that our eyes process upward of seven hundred thousand stimuli every second.

Psychologists have even theorized that the viewing of something at least three times has the same effect on the mind as one actual experience does. In other words, the visual component of communication is "the most powerful emotional connective tissue" we have when making contact with an individual, specifically a customer.[4]

Furthermore, research in communication has concluded that

1. retention increases 14–38% when visuals are used in conjunction with the spoken word. Would you like your customers to remember more of what you discussed in the sales process? Then use pictures and imagery.

2. goals are met 34% more often when visuals are used than when they are not. How would you like to close 34% more of your sales interviews? You can start by using pictures, imagery, sales materials, and other marketing pieces at the point of sale.

3. group consensus occurs 21% more often in meetings with visuals used than without. Wouldn't it be nice to get husbands and wives or business partners to agree more often during the sales process? The use of pictures will help you to accomplish this.

4. the time required to present a concept can be reduced by 40% with the use of visuals. Who out there wants to work smarter and not harder? Use pictures![5]

I am not asserting that the use of visuals, pictures, and imagery will correlate exactly to the percentages born out of past research. Each sales experience is unique, and the actual quantitative results will, no doubt, vary. But what is not in doubt is that the visual component of communication is powerful and a strong emotional conduit between the sales professional and the customer.

It is in the visual realm that people are right-brain-stimulated; imagery and our visual abilities reside in the right brain.[6] Therefore, physiologically speaking, our visual sense has a direct and clear connectivity to our emotional side, which also resides in the right-brain. Stimulate the visual centers of the customer's brain, and you stimulate their emotional centeredness as well by virtue of their neighboring origins. That is customer connectivity; the kind that increases the likelihood a sale is made and closed.

The Vocal Component

Not to be completely outdone by the power of visual connection, our vocals in communications form an emotional connection with customers as well.

Susan Berkley, TV-radio voiceover artist, author, and CEO of The Great Voice Company, Inc., a company that specializes in voice-mastery training for business and sales professionals, states: "Whenever you speak, the sound of your voice generates emotions, feelings, and gut-level reactions in other people. Some of these emotions are conscious and some are not, but these gut-level reactions form the basis for whether or not people like you, trust you, never take your call again, or decide to do business with you in the future."[7]

Dr. Lillian Glass, a speech consultant, studied the effects of speech on perceived attractiveness. Dr. Glass paired photographs of "good-looking" people, "average-looking" people, and people with facial deformities with tape-recorded voice samples that were "normal," mildly nasal-sounding, and severely nasal-sounding.

The results of her research showed that facially deformed subjects were considered more attractive when paired with a pleasant voice than when paired with a nasal-sounding voice. Conversely, good-looking subjects were considered less attractive, or unattractive, when paired with nasal-sounding speech. To coin a phrase used to sell a nationally advertised communications training program, "people do judge you by the way you speak."

Recalling Mehrabian's research, when all three components are working together in the delivery of a message, 38% of the effective power and impact of that message upon the customer's decision-making and behavior is in the vocal realm. But Mehrabian's research goes further in citing that when the visual component is not an element of the communication string (e.g., a telephone conversation), the overall impact percentages go up to 84% for vocals and 16% for the verbal realm.[8] There is no doubt: Vocals matter and they matter big with the customers and potential customers you come in contact with as a sales professional.

Have you ever tried to listen to someone whose vocals were cold, lifeless, monotone, with no energy or life? It is frustrating and boring for the listener. A good friend of mine, who has been in the insurance and financial services industry as an agent and sales manager for the past twenty years, calls this condition "ether breath." In other words, when someone with ether breath speaks, they put everyone to sleep. Don't be guilty of that error! Give your voice life—pause, raise, and lower your volume, dramatize your points, use intonation, and practice out loud to stimulate the right-brain and connect emotionally with the customer.

No matter how clear your logic is or how precise the words you use to express your ideas, "you will fail to convince people unless your beliefs and feelings show through in the way you use your words. This is vital in dealing with customers."[9] Vocals, although subordinate to the visual component in terms of persuasive power, matter tremendously in making a successful emotional connection with the customer.

The Verbal Component

Words, or verbal communications, are linear in nature, lacking the strong dynamic or emotional impact that visuals and vocals possess as connective tissue in communications. Yet, when coupled with good visuals and good vocals, verbal communication becomes a significant factor in a message being effectively delivered and a message being effectively received.

Our verbal communications are predominantly linked to left-brain functions. The left-brain is the factual side of our thinking, the quantifiable, statistical, and literal half of our minds. It is not the side where we are touched emotionally or motivated to act and do something.

The fact that our minds are separated into two hemispheres, the right and the left, does not suggest that they are not connected or are independent of the other when it comes to making decisions. The truth is, both hemispheres communicate and cross over, sharing stimuli and information as part of the normal function of the brain. So, to think that our verbals, by virtue of residing on the left side of brain, prevent any kind of emotional connection occurring is incorrect.

Psycholinguistics, the branch of study that looks at words and their effects on our minds and emotions, tells us that the verbal component of communication is an emotional link, or a connection—just perhaps not as strong a connection as our visual and vocal communication can be. But, nonetheless, verbal components strike a degree of emotional connection with customers. They are never neutral in their impact.

Carl Jung, the legendary Swiss psychologist, discovered that words are full of symbols. By a symbol, Jung meant that words spark an emotional reaction deep inside our subconscious. What a person says generates, at an unconscious level, certain feelings that are patterned over the years within our minds. For example, the words *denomination*, *sect*, and *cult* each carry a certain emotional attachment that stirs the mind when it is said.[10]

Advertisers know this to be true and, so, require the use of precise language in their marketing efforts, whether on television or in a printed medium. The use of positive words (e.g. interesting, strong, success, great, wonderful, glad, smart) grabs the customer's attention and can stir them to action and ultimately into buying. Whereas, negative words (e.g. can't, won't, never, difficult, maybe) conjure images and ideas that push people away, moving them in a direction mentally that is far from the closing of a sale.

So what does all this mean?

First of all, it means that to be a sales expert is to use visuals whenever communicating an idea and moving through the sales process. Get used to drawing concepts on paper, showing pictures, and utilizing company-produced sales pieces to stimulate the customer's mind to act. A picture is worth a thousand words!

Secondly, it means that vocals matter—perhaps not as strongly in terms of the emotional impact visuals stir within the customer, but they matter significantly. Listen to your voice even though it may seem silly or even painful for you to do. Just do it!

Listen for detractors. How does your voice sound to you? Is it friendly? Does it sound squeaky or nasally? Is your speech slow or too fast? How you say things matters a lot. The sales professional willing to listen to their recorded voice is the one who is willing to take their profession and sales to the next level.

Lastly, your words, or verbal content, do matter in making an emotional connection with the customer. How is the content of your sales conversations? Have you ever scripted out what you are used to saying and sat down to read it—really read it—for what it says and how it might sound? It is hard work, and it takes time to script out things. But if you want to take your profession, the sales craft, to the next level, there are some hard things that have to be done in order to achieve such distinction.

Do you use power robbers—like "um," "you know," "basically," or "and what not"—in your speech? They are like viruses attached to your verbal content. They weaken your credibility and are static against the verbal message you are sending to the customer.

Do you use positive language such as "we," "us," "together," "process," "benefit," "investment," "assured," "help," et cetera? Such language is inviting and draws the customer toward you and toward the sale.

Do you speak in a manner that appeals to the customer--a manner that is focused on them and their concerns; a manner that feeds the egocentric nature of people and touches their individualistic senses to feel important and feel special?

Or instead, do you speak in a company-centric way, that is, do you speak "at" the customer about the company and the product with language that does not relate to them personally, that doesn't address the benefit to them of why they should buy from you? If so, you will quickly discover your error as customers begin to go elsewhere to buy from other salespeople who will give them what they are looking for; a positive experience when buying something.

People are visual, vocal, and verbal—in that order—when it comes to the impact, or emotional connectivity, a message makes with the listener. Since sales is a contact sport, it behooves the sales professional to heed the realities of our natural psychological makeup and to use clear imagery, variety in vocal usage, and positive words or verbals in all conversations. The combined effect on a sales conversation's ability to persuade the customer to buy will make the difference between success and failure.

CHAPTER SEVEN: KEY NOTES

People Connect Visually, Vocally, and Verbally

* All three components of communication possess an inherent weight or power to influence. All three have an intrinsic impact to persuade, influence, and emotionally connect with the customer.

* The impact hierarchy is as follows: visual, vocal, then verbal (the emotional connective tissue in communications).

1. Visual Communication

    A. Retention, goals, consensus, and time are all positively affected by the use of visuals in the sales process.

    B. Visuals stimulate right-brain functions.

2. Vocal Communication

    A. The sound of our voice stimulates emotions within others.

    B. Logic and the use of words without good, convincing vocals will not convince customers of your message.

3. Verbal Communication

    A. Words alone are linear in nature—they are not as convincing apart from proper vocals and visuals.

    B. Psycholinguists tell us that verbal communication does make an emotional connection with other people. Therefore, it not only matters *what* you say; it matters *how* you say things as well.

* What does this all mean for the sales professional?

    1. Use visuals in all your sales strategies. The wise sales professional doesn't try to talk someone into a sale. Instead, they listen them into the sale using pictures, graphs, and visually effective marketing materials.

    2. Have the courage to record and listen to your vocals. Be critical and adjust. Pay particular attention to tone, tempo, and volume.

    3. Perfect practice makes perfect—get rid of verbal power robbers. The one sure way to do this is to script out your presentations.

PART II

Understanding Value and How It Is Perceived

The focus of the first half of this book was on the general nature and principles of human dynamics that are in play when the customer decides to buy something. The fact of our emotional centeredness—our natural tendencies toward being judgmental, resistant, egocentric, individualistic, and visual/vocal/verbal in our hierarchies of communication when buying—proves that people base decisions first on emotions and later justify those emotional decisions with logic.

Emotionally centered and logically dispersed, the centerpiece of how we process and decide to buy, is a key understanding to achieving sales success on a personal and professional level when it comes to production and sales-revenue growth.

In the next segment of this book, we will build on our understanding of people and their emotionally centered natures to gain a practical understanding of what value is and how the customer perceives it.

Consumers are looking for value. Whether they are conscious of this fact or not at the point of sale is irrelevant. What is relevant is that sales professionals should provide the customer with what they want...value. If you don't, someone else will.

"Value is in the eye of the beholder."

DIANE LASALLE AND TERRY A. BRITTON
PRICELESS[1]

Chapter Eight

Why Buy? Understanding Price and Value

In the insurance and financial services industry, I often hear sales professionals declare grudgingly, "It's all about price these days. I don't care what anyone says...price rules!"

I understand why they say such things, especially, for example, when a competitive auto-premium quote comes in $100 less than your own quote. All too often, at that point, we quickly end the sales conversation, wave the white flag, and politely smile, wishing the customer Godspeed while secretly hoping a year from now the tables will be turned on the competition, and they will have to raise their rates above ours.

Price Does Matter

Now I realize that scenarios like this happen every day in the life of an agent or financial services sales professional. I also understand that *price does matter*. It is undeniable; most customers are shopping around for the *best* price. But all too often we, as sales experts, get hooked into the classic competitive sales conversation where price is the main topic of discussion and differentiation.

The truth of the matter is, price is the easiest thing for a competitor to replicate or undercut. All it takes to be competitive in the price arena is a sale sign or a pricing gun along with the resolve to live under tighter margins.[2] That might work in the world of commodity products but not in the highly competitive arena of insurance and financial services.

In fact, few things that can be purchased are true commodities. Most products and services have differentiating features and value propositions attached to them that simply are not effectively communicated to the customer. Therein lies the real issue we must battle as sales professionals: communicating value.

If You Live by Price, You Die by Price

Too often, many sales professionals approach the art of the sale one-dimensionally, focused on a number rather than communicating value. Consequently, we have raised a generation of consumers and created market segments that have never been sold on value, have never heard a value-based sales conversation, and appreciate nothing more than the thought of a low price and the opportunity to shop it every year against the competition.

"The art of persuasion is paradoxical. The more we attempt to persuade people, the more they tend to resist us. But the more we attempt to

*understand them and create value for them, the
more they tend to persuade themselves."*

RON WILLINGHAM
INTEGRITY SELLING FOR THE 21ST CENTURY[3]

It isn't until we communicate value that we
can combat the notion of a lower price being the
better buy for the customer.

Price Is Not the *Whole* Matter

Price is not the sole factor in determining why
people buy. In fact, in the great majority of buying scenarios, price is not even the primary reason for why people buy a particular product or
service at all. It can't be, or else there wouldn't
be sunglasses for sale at the local mall kiosk for
$10 a piece while in the same mall, designer sun-
glasses are sold for $200 a piece and higher in a
brand-name storefront. How can that be if price
is the primary guiding force in shaping our decisions to choose to buy something?

Think about the times when you have purchased something, particularly something of a
significant nature or substantial dollar amount.
Whatever the item, now ask yourself these questions: "What was it that moved me to buy it? Why
did I buy that particular item, from that particular person, at that particular place?" This becomes an even more instructive exercise when
taking into consideration those purchases where
you actually had a choice about what to buy and
from whom and where to buy it from.

Think about it. Break it down. Certainly, price is a factor. But was price the primary factor for you in deciding? For example, if it was a car that comes to mind, ask yourself, "Why that model car versus another? Why did I buy the color I bought? Why did I buy from that dealership?"

Or if you are thinking of a home you purchased, "Why that home? Why that neighborhood? Why that style of house? Why did you stay with a particular realtor?"

And if you say to yourself, "It is because *the price was right*...it really had nothing to do with anything else," then consider this: Isn't the statement "the price was right" just another way of saying "the price was worth it"? This is what value is all about anyway—worth!

In my training sessions, I ask sales professionals questions like, "What is it that causes you, when in the role of a consumer and buyer, to purchase a particular thing from a particular person at a particular place?" Without exception, the list of responses as to why they buy is dominated with statements like "a friendly, knowledgeable salesperson...a nice environment...a salesperson that is not pushy and who cares about me...a salesperson I can trust...one who doesn't make me feel stupid and who lets me decide...not a high-pressure salesperson...one who makes me feel comfortable and special."

Invariably, price does get added to the list of reasons for buying. But in all my years of training and asking sales professionals about their own buying experiences, not once has price been the lead reason given. In fact, it rarely appears in the top half of the list of reasons why they buy.

Independent research with investor-buyers further validates customer motives for buying in listing the top six factors people value when choosing to work with a particular financial services advisor and company: (1) understands my situation, (2) educates me, (3) respects my assets, (4) solves my problems, (5) monitors my progress, and (6) keeps in touch.[4]

So what are we to make of all this talk about price and the reasons why people buy? If we consider once again the emotional centeredness of people and the basic human need to connect with other people emotionally rather than on the rational cognitive level, then we can begin to build a template for sales techniques, marketing, and sales training that works.

Sales is a contact sport. People need validation and connection, and that is achieved through emotional connection and value communicated and perceived. "Incorporating emotion into the value equation works because it's naturally how our thinking and feeling minds function."[5] And when something has enough value, people will pay just about anything to have it. On the other hand, without value communicated, there's not much of a reason for people to buy.[6] If we don't deliver on value, customers will go where they can get it: from the competition.

People Are Looking for Value

Value is why people buy from one particular person or place versus another. Value is why some people are willing to spend more on something knowing they can get it cheaper elsewhere. It is why people become loyal customers. People want value. They are looking for it!

But what exactly is this thing called value? How would you define what value is or does? By strict definition, value is the relationship between price and the benefits of having a product or service. Value is getting what you want relative to price. Even more simply said, value answers this question in the customer's mind: Is the price worth it? It is our reason for buying.

Value Is a Personal Matter

Value is different from person to person. What I value, what I feel is important to me, and what needs I have are very personal and unique. My thoughts, desires, circumstances, and life experiences are highly subjective and exclusive. They shape my beliefs and value system. Therefore, the value I have for a particular product and service will vary in comparison to another person's sense of value under similar circumstances.

For example, a bowl of rice to a downtrodden and starving man has vastly different value than it would to the man whose belly is content and full. Need and desire differ among individuals and vary in strength and impact from person to person.

The point to be understood is that you will never sell well unless you first ask good probing questions of your customers—questions that reveal who they are, what they are looking for, what is important to them, and the emotional reason for why they would buy your product or service in the first place. Until the sales professional uncovers the emotional criterion, or reasons, for buying they cannot offer the customer any value or any worth relative to the price being asked.

The Emotional Criteria for Buying

Consider the emotional reasons why people might buy life insurance. Some buy it for the *peace of mind* of knowing that if they were to die, the home and lifestyle that they worked so hard to provide for their families won't be in jeopardy.

Other people buy it for *a good conscience*, knowing they have done the right and good thing for loved ones who are depending upon them. Sometimes the emotional criteria for buying is *to keep things private*—for instance, to keep the government and the IRS out of the picture by making sure that the taxes and debts are paid and the family business or farm is passed on to loved ones hassle free.

Then again, some people buy life insurance for *the emotional need of advancing their ambitions* in business. For example, securing a large commercial loan for business expansion may be contingent upon meeting the life insurance requirements of the lender or business. Whatever the product, whatever the service being sold, the reason people buy is first and foremost an emotional one.

Value truly is in the eye of the beholder.

Value Is a Perception

Value is not only a personal matter, but it is a perception as well. Perception has to do with the union of awareness, understanding, and belief wrapped into a single impression of something or someone. As height, depth, and width form our cognitive perceptions of our three-dimensional world, awareness, understanding, and belief form our perceptions of value. Each component—like height, depth, and width—are distinct and possess their own characteristics. Yet, as inseparable forces, they form the whole of our sense of value.

In other words, without the customer being made aware of how a product or service is different, without the customer having at least a basic understanding of how it can work and what it is, and without a customer's belief that a product or service can meet or exceed personal wants or needs, there is no value perceived.

"Value Perceived Is Value Received"

For the customer to perceive value they must *receive* the message of value—that is, value must be effectively communicated, or delivered, in order to be *perceived* at all. Otherwise, the customer will never see the benefits of ownership for themselves.

Remember, people are egocentric in nature. Therefore, value is inextricably tied to their perception of what something *does* for them, or the bottom-line personal benefit that they will get from buying something from you. That is at the core of "value perceived." Plenty of good service businesses and excellent products have failed in the marketplace for want of good communicators: sales professionals who understand the linkage between "what something is" and "what something does" for the customer and the need to communicate the two.

Value perceived by the customer answers the simple question, "Am I getting something others aren't getting?" Or, better yet, "Am I getting all that they say I am going to get for what I am willing to pay?"

If all a salesperson does is focus on price during the sales conversation, then the product being sold will naturally be perceived as a commodity by the consumer...something that is easily comparable to the competition's product with the only difference being the price.

That is the struggle sales experts face every day--the struggle between commoditization and value based selling. This is particularly evident in the automobile and homeowners insurance industry where insurance has been commoditized to the point where the consumer sees no differentiating feature other than if the price offered is higher or lower than a competitor's price.

Consequently, in the majority of situations where price is the focus of the sales conversation, the consumer naturally defers to the mental exercise of comparing your price to that of the other guy. As a result, the salesperson can count on closing the sale only if they are cheaper than the competition...and they can expect to lose the sale if they are higher.

Why? Because, when price becomes the focus of a sales conversation, it conditions the customer's thinking and becomes the catalyst that triggers the impulse to buy from you or not. This is hardly a recipe for longevity and success in the sales profession...and it ultimately does nothing in terms of serving the customer's best interests.

The truth is, auto and homeowners insurance is not a commodity product at all. There are differentiating features other than a cheaper price that make these products a good buy for the consumer.

Contained within every policy are benefits which, if communicated effectively to the customer, will build a sense of value in their mind beyond the issue of how much it will cost. Unfortunately, what has been the practice of many insurance and financial sales professionals in the past, to sell on price, has become one of the major obstacles to sales success for the future.

As a result, many sales professionals now find themselves with no other alternative strategy than to reduce margins and cut expenses in order to compete. They have fallen into a trap of their own making—selling on price and not selling on value.

Sales Professionals Are Responsible for the Right Perceptions

If you sell the customer on price, then the customer will leave you for price. Why? Because the prospect of a *cheaper price as the better option* is the perception most sales professionals build upon and communicate to consumers when in sales conversations.

Once again, perception is the inseparable unity of awareness, understanding, and belief that a consumer has in a product or service. The mistake sales professionals all too often make is in communicating wrong perceptions to the customer, wrong perceptions about the competition and their lower price, wrong perceptions that cheaper is better, and wrong perceptions about value and what it really means to the customer.

Therefore, it is the responsibility of every sales professional to build right perceptions. Those right perceptions are built through effective communication of the elements that customers *value*. As sales experts, we need to be effective communicators who understand what value is and the need for it to be received into the mind of the consumer.

Value Is a Price

Value is a personal matter, value is a perception, and value is a price. Please note closely that I did not say that value is *the* price. Value is expressed, or made apparent and manifest in a number we commonly refer to as price.

Price is the quantitative measure or expression of what someone is willing to give in order to get something. Alone, it is a sterile thing—something clinical and precise that registers with the left side of the brain but builds upon the emotions of the right side of the brain. Price, if communicated properly, is a gauge for value—a measuring stick of sorts.

What gives price meaning and relevance is all the emotional benefits perceived by the customer in owning a product or service. So another definition for price can be "the quantitative measure of the emotional value perceived by the customer."

Supporting this definition is the fact that value is perceived only when value is received by way of effective sales communication.

"Price is no more than a function of perceived value, which itself is derived from our feelings of how important a product is to us. In other words, price is a function of emotion. It is definitely not a function of any logical formula."

DAVID FREEMANTLE
WHAT CUSTOMERS LIKE ABOUT YOU[7]

Value Is a Package

Value is also a package; that is, value is something that is made up of several parts that include price. So not only is it a personal matter, a perception and an expression of value in a thing called a price, but value is synergy between the sum of its parts.

It is a symphony of the facts and features of a product or service, its people, and its place, harmonizing with the emotional wants and needs of the customer. It is a score written in the left-brain and performed in the right-brain.

When I was a Boy Scout, one of the first merit badges I worked toward earning was the Firemanship Merit Badge. To earn it, one of the basic concepts that I had to understand was how fire is started or sustained.

I learned that three components make up fire: heat, fuel, and oxygen. Traditionally, the relationship of these three components is depicted by a triangle with each component represented on a side of the triangle and the word fire centered within the triangle. The graphic purpose of this fire triangle was to teach us by visual aid that if one of the components depicted on the side of the fire triangle were to be taken out of the "fire equation," then a fire will not start or sustain itself.

Similarly, value is made up of relationships between various components in order for it to be perceived and received cognitively and emotionally by the customer. These components are the price, the product, the person (or sales professional), and the place where people buy.

Take one of these components out of the "value equation" and the perception of value begins to diminish and eventually extinguish. To visualize the components of price, product, the person, and the place and how the relationship between them builds value within the mind of the customer, I've constructed The Value Diamond, which I will explain in the following chapter.

CHAPTER EIGHT: KEY NOTES

Why Buy? Understanding Price and Value

* Price does matter, but it is not the *whole* matter when it comes to selling and value.

    1. Price is the easiest thing for the competition to replicate or undercut...value, on the other hand, is not easily replicated.

* If you live by Price, you will die by price.

    1. Selling by price attracts and creates a certain type of customer base, one that appreciates nothing more than a low price and the opportunity to shop it against the competition.

* Price is all too often the scapegoat for why a sale is not closed.

    1. Research and observation prove that buying is emotional first and rational second.

* People are looking for value. If sales professionals don't deliver on value, customers will go where they can get it: from the competition.

    1. Value is a personal matter.

A. It varies from person to person.

B. A customer's personal emotional criteria for buying (value system) must be leveraged in order to close the sale.

2. Value is a perception.
   A. Value perceived is value received.
      (1) Customers perceive value only when they receive value. That is, customers will never see the value in a product or service unless the sales professional effectively communicates value to them.

3. Value is a price.
   A. Value is not *the* price.
   B. Price is the quantitative measure or expression of what someone is willing to give in order to get something.

4. Value is a package.
   A. Value has its component parts: price, product, person, and place.
   B. Each component adds to the customer perception of value. This concept is depicted in The Value Diamond.

"Selling is transacting value."

MACK HANAN AND PETER KARP
COMPETING ON VALUE[1]

The Value Diamond

(A Template for Marketing, Sales, and Training)

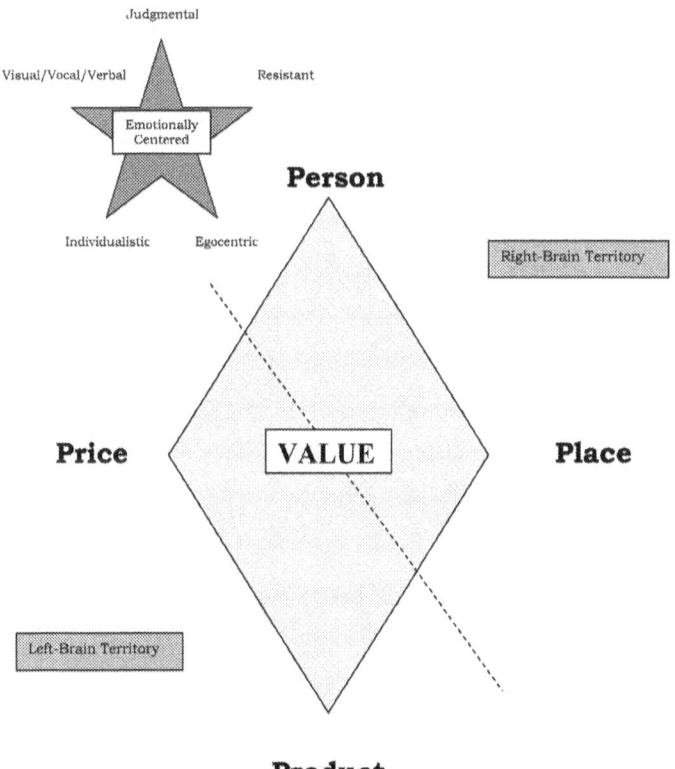

Judgmental

Visual/Vocal/Verbal   Resistant

Emotionally Centered

Person

Individualistic   Egocentric

Right-Brain Territory

Price   VALUE   **Place**

Left-Brain Territory

Product

Sell the Whole Package

CHAPTER NINE

The Value Diamond

Previously, we examined how people are emotionally centered creatures by nature and that our tendencies are to decide on emotion first and rationalize our decisions second. Thus, we are emotionally centered and logically dispersed creatures. Each emotional decision is supported by logic only to the degree that it validates our choices to buy (logically dispersed).

We have also looked at how this dominant-recessive relationship between emotion and rational thinking plays into our natural biases in terms of being *judgmental, resistant* to the sales process, *egocentric, individualistic* and *visual, vocal, and verbal.*

People Feel First and Rationalize Later

Our emotional centeredness is what drives the decision-making process and shapes our perceptions of the world. Over a century ago, Dr. William James of Harvard University stated that when the emotions and will are in conflict, "the emotions rule the day...Emotions always precede fact in the human brain response. People feel first and rationalize later."[2]

Our ability to perceive and sense value during the sales process is, therefore, subject to the same dominant-recessive relationship between emotion and rational thinking. Value is a perception whose roots are anchored in both the emotional and the rational. The error commonly committed by sales professionals is that they often lead with the rational and give little or no effort to communicating the emotional to customers. As a result, untold sales opportunities are missed, customers leave with needs unfulfilled and sales professionals grow frustrated and discouraged at not closing the sales conversation.

In The Value Diamond, we will first examine the one value component that often dominates a sales conversation and a sales professional's strategy in closing with a customer: price. It is the one reason why products and services ultimately become commoditized in the consumer's mind when buying.

The Price

"Commoditization thinking" is largely an industry-created phenomenon. Customers define, sense, and perceive value by what sales professionals communicate to them. If the only differentiating feature communicated to the customer is price, then that is the frame of reference the customer will use in deciding to buy or not to buy. Hence, commoditization thinking prevails.

The insurance and financial services industry has 1-800 phone numbers and Internet sites that are used to sell insurance products every day, thus, reinforcing the public's sense that what we sell is a commodity instead of a value-added product or service.

By value-added product or service, I mean that a *good price* means more than getting a cheaper or better price for something over another competitor's offer. Value-added is the very definition of what "good" is in the *good price* statement a customer may make. It encompasses the intangible and tangible benefits connected to a purchase and unless value is communicated effectively, it will not be perceived or connected with the purchase price.

It is a fact that distribution channels like these are valid streams for connecting with the market and those customers who wish to shop by phone or Internet. Undeniably, customer needs are met and market demands are appeased by the use of such channels.

However, these channels do not make for a loyal customer base because of the emotional detachment they inherently create between the seller and the buyer. This emotional detachment attracts a certain kind of customer, the kind that is, again, conditioned to see insurance products simply as a commodity. The result is a transient customer base that is attracted by price and retained only by price.

Once the competition lowers their price with the "sticker gun," that price-conscious customer becomes tomorrow's defecting client. Companies that predominantly sell this way structure their business models and expectations on high customer-defection rates and high new-business volume.

But even those companies who model their distribution systems for high defection and high new-business rates are recognizing the business need to establish stronger customer connections. It is just too hard and unprofitable strategically to get the business "in the door" and "on the books" to only see it run "out the door" because of a focus on a cheaper price. That is why many of the companies that traditionally sold on price are beginning to build strategies to help the consumer see the added value in buying from them.

It is not that these companies have abandoned their distribution channels of telephone, Internet sites, and direct mail; it is just that they have realized the power of building relationships and connecting emotionally with the consumer...and the effect customer loyalty has on retention and bottom-line profits.

Therefore, companies have begun to train their call-center sales force and telemarketing cadre on how to present price, when to present price, and how to counter objections about price with value-added language. They have also begun training their agency distribution channels on how to speak more of the emotional language of the customer and to uncover the emotional criteria for why a person would buy a particular product from a particular person at a particular store or agency.

Price Is Predominantly a Left-Brain Function

Still, almost daily I hear sales professionals having one-dimensional conversations with customers that are solely focused on who has the lower price. Once again, it merits noting that *price is merely the quantitative measure or expression of what someone is willing to pay in order to have or get something.*

Alone, price is sterile, clinical, precise, and rational. It is something that registers on the left side of the brain where analysis and quantified, rational thinking occurs. It does not reside in that part of the mind where decisions are made and emotions rule without some other sales dynamic to bridge the gap.

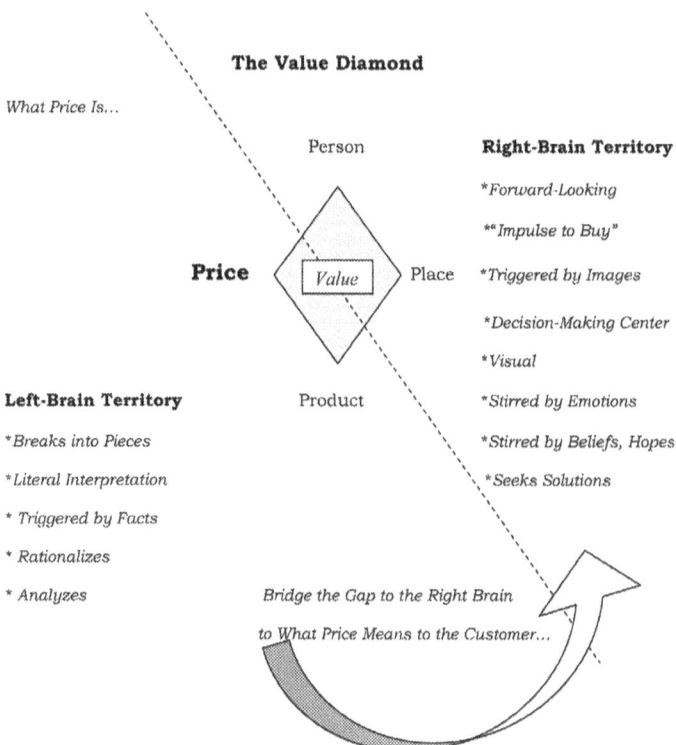

The Value Diamond

What Price Is...

Person

Right-Brain Territory

Forward-Looking

""Impulse to Buy"

Price | *Value* | Place

Triggered by Images

Decision-Making Center

Visual

Left-Brain Territory | Product

Stirred by Emotions

Breaks into Pieces

Stirred by Beliefs, Hopes

Literal Interpretation

Seeks Solutions

* *Triggered by Facts*

* *Rationalizes*

* *Analyzes*

Bridge the Gap to the Right Brain
to What Price Means to the Customer...

Price, then, is a measure or expression of value much like Fahrenheit and Celsius are common numeric indexes used to gauge heat. They are precise; numeric in nature and literal by interpretation and are what naturally registers and appeals to the left-brain and not the right-brain. Consequently, price lacks the inherent power to move the customer to buy when not presented in a fashion that fails to link it to the right-brain... where emotions reside.

Normally, as a measure or expression of value, price is set by the home office. Such is the case for the insurance and financial services industry where the price of products and services that are sold cannot be changed or negotiated by frontline sales professionals. Therefore, without the ability to price-cut, the insurance professional must become much more skilled than the average sales professional in the art of communicating *value* effectively.

By formulating a bridging strategy to the emotional right-brain, a sales professional can move the customer beyond the realm of price as a simple, literal expression to an expression of worth by stirring the emotions. This bridging strategy begins with uncovering what it is the customer wants and expects when buying something.

How Should Price be Presented?

Price is a component of The Value Diamond and because it is an element of a customer's perception of value, there must be a way and a proper time that price can be effectively presented to bridge the emotional centers of the right brain.

So, then, how should price be presented? First of all, it should never be presented alone, meaning that it should never be presented without an emotionally bridging thought or idea (e.g. emotional reason for buying) connected to it. This is one of the most common mistakes made by sales professionals.

Good sales probing of the customer should uncover the emotional criteria specific to a customer's wants, needs, and concerns. Connecting that emotional thought to the price bridges the gap and crosses over to the right-brain, where emotion and the impulse to decide and act reside.

Consider what is happening in the mind of a customer that hears from the sales professional, "The cost of auto insurance for you is $400 every six months." Or, worse yet, consider what the customer is thinking when they hear, "The cost of auto insurance for you is *only* $400 every six months."

First of all, customers begin to process the statement about price in their left-brain, the quantitative, rational, and literal side of the mind. Next, they begin to seek for relevance, that is, they begin to search for what the price means to them personally. And without a strong bridging strategy to the right-brain, the idea or thought of price remains a left-brain process--something that is sterile, cold, without the natural emotional attachment that drives every customer's impulse to buy.

In regard to the often used statement: "The cost of auto insurance for you is *only* $400," my observations have been that the customer can be subtly insulted by the use of the word *only*. Why? It is because customers are perceptive; to presume they don't recognize such a weak sales *technique* designed to manipulate their thinking that the price is a "good" one is a mistake. It assumes the customer is gullible and not sophisticated enough to make that decision on their own...instead they have to be told.

The customer can decide whether something is a good price or not on their own, manipulation techniques aren't necessary. Only when sales professionals communicate price along with the emotional reason for buying can a stronger, and more ethical, value proposition be gained within the mind of the customer.

Price and Relevance

If price is benign and neutral by itself, a quantitative thing that is sterile, factual, and without meaning when considered alone, then it must have something to compare itself to in order to give it meaning and relevance.

Consider the following:

Question: How do I know that this line is crooked?

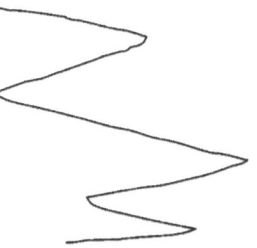

Answer: When it is juxtaposed next to a straight line.

Too often, what price is juxtaposed next to in order to give it meaning or relevance is the competitor's price. That is because sales professionals often present price without a bridging statement that ties it to the emotional right-brain where the impulse to buy resides.

You see, if all that is offered is the price, then the customer naturally has no other option but to mentally make the comparison with what the competition is asking. This becomes an even easier task for the customer when the product is already viewed incorrectly as a commodity, as in the case with auto insurance. Such a mental exercise on the part of the customer does not create a strong value-added connection to the buying impulse.

Thus, if the competitor's price (the standard used to define a price's relevance) is lower than your own price, then the customer understands your price to be a sacrifice, something that they have to *give-up* in order to get what you are selling. Value, at this juncture, simply becomes a question of who has the cheaper price. Any other benefits associated with the product or service being sold gets clouded or is overlooked without ever being appreciated by the customer. Therefore, no strong desire is created to buy other than the desire to get the cheapest price for something.

Instead, what sales professionals need to do is to *get the customer thinking in a new way* that has them saying to themselves, "This [great service or product support, etc.] is what I *get* if I go with your product or service and pay the asking price." It is a different way of thinking that is subtle in application, yet very powerful in determining whether a sale is closed or not.

Change the Reference Point

The best way to steer customer thinking toward value is to *change the primary reference point* used in defining value. As we have outlined, the most common reference point customers use for defining value and giving relevance to a price is the competitor's price in comparison.

A new reference point that's different from the price comparison way of thinking focuses first on what you, the sales professional, have to offer in addition to what is being sold. That is, in order to change or shift the momentum of customer thinking away from price comparisons alone, the sales professional must become adept at replacing the price comparison standard with another standard, one that uses benefits of ownership over the cost of something in order to compel people to buy.

Thus, the only alternative available to the sales professional to combat a competitor's lower price is to communicate higher value. Simply put, it is higher value that is the new reference point to be used.

Compete on Lower Price with Higher Value

When it comes to presenting price, always bridge the emotions of the right-brain with a value statement that relates to the customer's emotional reason for buying. That is how price becomes linked to value, or perceptions of value, by the customer.

Therefore, rather than stating, "The cost of auto insurance for you is $400 every six months," finish the sentence with an emotional bridge or connector. For example:

> "The cost of auto insurance for you and your family is $400 every six months. What that means is that you have the peace of mind knowing that if you were to get into an accident, you, your wife and children, along with any passengers that may be riding with you, won't have to worry if the car will be fixed-- or have to scramble to get a ride to work or school while the car is being repaired.

And if you, or any of your children, are hurt in the accident--you don't have to worry about in-network...out-of-network issues. That's a hassle and not something you want to deal with when an accident has occurred. You can rest assured that you'll be protected in that regard. And if you have any questions about your bill, or your coverage, we're here for you...a phone call away....easy, no hassles, just dial our 1-800 number and you'll speak to a live person about what you need...not some frustrating recorded message that asks you to leave a message like most other places have you do."

Or

"The cost is $400 in order to have the peace of mind knowing that you'll have the storage capacity to process every transaction locally, as you mentioned you needed, and to make sure your customer orders are retrievable, quickly and easily, without error, saving you time, money, and a lot of heartache in the long run."

Or

"Tom, you can rest assured that if you decide on this life insurance, your family will be able to live in the home you worked so hard to provide for them and that their lives will be disrupted financially as little as possible. In order to do so, it will cost you $400 a year.

But look at what you have done…you've taken care of your loved ones and made it possible for them to continue on in their same school, with their same friends, in the home that they were born in."

However the price statement is worded, the key to properly presenting price is to connect on an emotional level with the customer. That is how you bridge customer thinking from the left-brain to the right-brain where the impulse to buy resides. This is the smarter and more effective way to present price and to close the sale.

"Price is what you pay. Value is what you get."

WARREN BUFFET

If we continue to present price improperly, the customer will continue to dictate the terms of its relevance by comparing it to the competitions' price. That is not a strong or persuasive emotional connection. The better way is to always present price with the emotional reason for buying attached to it. That's how value is perceived…and that is how value is received in the mind of the customer.

When Should Price Be Presented?

This brings us to the other issue at hand: When is the proper time to present price? Naturally, my response is: Not until the customer perceives value. The arguments remain the same as before: If value is not communicated effectively and perceived by the customer...then the price is not ready to be shared with the customer. Otherwise, price becomes something the customer has to "give up" rather than something they pay to "get" what they want or need.

I understand that customers can get anxious, impatient, and downright direct about wanting to know the price right away before any value discussions can be held. It will happen. In those instances, I suggest that you develop a strategy that defers the sharing of the price until the time is right to do so. It *pays* to be prepared...literally!

Customer: "What's the cost?"

> **Sales Professional:** "I understand that price is important, and I'll be happy to share that with you. Before I do, I'd like to make sure I've explained to your satisfaction our services and what we offer our clients who choose to do business with us, if that is okay. How does that sound?...Great!"

The specific verbiage may vary, but the fact is, have a plan for when the premature price question is posed. If the customer persists, by all means, give them what they want. You don't want them doubting or thinking you are hiding anything.

Just be sure to always connect price to an emotional reason for buying no matter how brief that [value-added] statement is. And if you haven't had an opportunity to sufficiently probe the customer to uncover their particular emotional reasons for buying, simply connect the price to some of the most common reasons that you are aware of already.

Know your customers, your market segments, and your products and services; then ask yourself what the common emotional reasons are for why people buy from you. List them out, memorize them; they will serve you well in the long run.

"Preparation is the price you pay to get the price you deserve."

LEN SERAFINO
SALES TALK[3]

Furthermore, on this issue of when to present price, I am sometimes accused of advocating deceptive sales strategies in recommending that the answer be deferred until value is established. That assertion is completely inaccurate. What I am advocating is that sales professionals *ask* to defer the answer in order to fully communicate value to the customer.

Buying a product or service is so much more than just price. There may be issues of delivery time, reliability, quality, relevance, and appropriateness that need to be discussed with the customer in order for them to make the best decision they can for themselves.

To automatically react to their premature requests for price will, most likely, cloud or bias their ability to make an educated and prudent choice for themselves. Bottom line: Tell the customer the price, but try to do so after you have effectively communicated value to them. Otherwise, give them what they ask for...the price!"

**Price Stated + Emotional Reason for Buying
= Value Communicated
Value Communicated = Value Received**

One last thing in regard to price: An effective means of accentuating the value proposition is to break price down into reasonably smaller, understandable amounts. This helps the customer gain a better appreciation and perspective for the value you are offering.

For example:

"Tom, the cost is $400 in order for you to have the peace of mind knowing that you'll have the storage capacity to process every transaction locally, as you mentioned you needed, and to make sure your customer orders are retrievable, quickly and easily and without error, saving you time, money, and a lot of heartache in the long run.

"That is a little more than a dollar a day to have the assurance of knowing that your customer accounts are available to you at the press of a button and that you won't have to worry about accounting errors and customer complaints as before. Don't you think that is worth it?"

Or

"Tom, in order to assure that your family will be able to live in the home you worked so hard to provide for them, and that their lives are disrupted financially as little as possible if you were to die today, it will cost $400 a year to have this life insurance.

That is less than $35 a month: essentially the cost of a pizza every weekend in order to have the peace of mind knowing that Mary, Lindsay, and Sara won't have to worry about where to live or how the bills will be paid with the income loss that would follow your death.

And, correct me if I'm wrong, but you and Mary both stated at the beginning of our conversation that keeping the house and being able to keep the girls here in school is very important to you. Is that correct? That is what is being proposed here, the ability to take care of that concern you have for your family. Does this sound like a good plan for what you are looking for?"

In life insurance sales, it can be quite evident what a customer's emotional criterion is for buying. The second example above assumes that a thorough discussion—where adequate probing of needs was done—already took place with the customer.

In this case, the husband wanted to make sure his wife and children could pay off the mortgage if he were to die. Assuming the solution is a $100,000 term life insurance policy, price must be presented properly so that the customer will weigh it against the benefits of ownership.

Those benefits of ownership are having the *peace of mind* knowing that the family can pay the house off after the loss of income due to death, the *relief from worry*, and the idea that it will *make things easier* and cause *less of an emotional upheaval* with life insurance money available. It is a subtle strategy but very powerful in terms of persuading the customer to consider price as a means of getting something of emotional importance, not as a proposition where you have to give something up.

If what you offer doesn't meet the customer's emotional criteria or need for buying, so be it! You should never force someone to buy something that does not satisfy their needs and value system, plain and simple.

Value is a package, a package depicted graphically in The Value Diamond and that begins first with the idea of *how* to present price and *when* to present price.

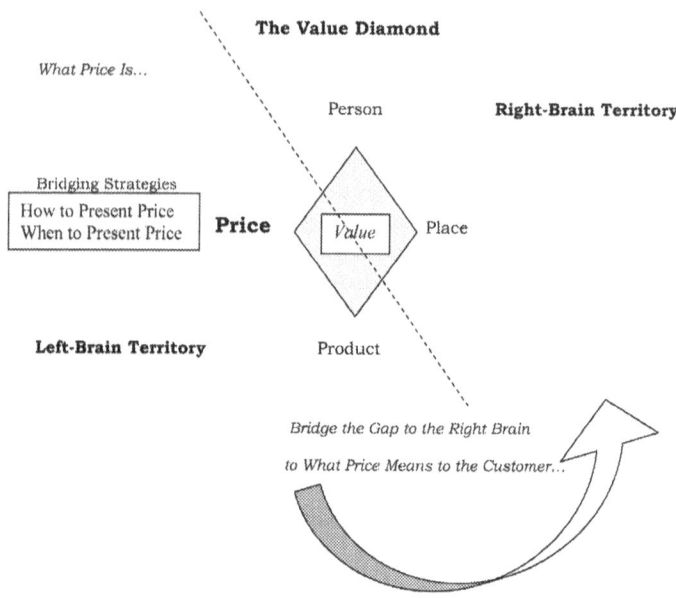

Value is also derived, or perceived, by way of the product. In the same manner as with price, many sales professionals fail to properly articulate product and service features in language the customer connects with emotionally.

Often, sales professionals speak in factual, clinical, product-centered ways when presenting their sales solutions. The art of sales is to speak in benefit-rich, customer-centered language when speaking of product.

The Product

Every product and service contains features, or facts, characteristic to them that need to be communicated. These facts do not speak to *what something does* but to *what something is about.*

They tell us about a product and are, thus, left-brain in nature, as is price.

Features Tell and Benefits Sell

Product features are just as benign and unemotional as price when they stand alone. And, similar to price, there is the common sales error often made to "laundry list" the features (facts) of a product while failing to connect it to the emotional reasons of what a product *does* to fulfill customer needs.

Speaking to what something does for the customer is termed "beneficial language." Failure to speak "beneficially" about your product results in a failure to connect emotionally to a customer. And, remember, people are emotionally centered creatures and are moved to buy in that realm first and to justify that decision afterward by logic. People do not buy because of what something *is*; they buy for what something *does* for them.

A simple exercise that I often take sales professionals through in order to help them make the transition from speaking in a company-focused, product-centered manner to a more customer-centered way begins with a discussion of the features offered in a product. We then translate those features into customer-centered, beneficial language.

The result: A way of speaking to the customer that touches not only the logical left-brain but also speaks to the emotional right-brain is developed. The features touch upon the factual side (left), and the benefits touch upon the feeling side (right) of our brains.

"What's your product? What feeling will your customer walk away with? Peace of mind? Power? Love? What is he really buying when he buys from you? The truth is, nobody's interested in the commodity. People buy feelings."

MICHAEL GERBER
THE E-MYTH[4]

There are two ways to effectively communicate product and services to customers. One way is the "old" way: "the feature way," if you will. It is a sales conversation and belief system that strives to *tell* the customer all about what the product *is*. It focuses on the facts and warranties of a product rather than what it can *do* for someone.

It is a sales philosophy of the left-brain, where facts, figures, and features reside in order to argue their point for the sale. Most of the time, this is how sales professionals sell, particularly when their product and service is "factually" superior to the competition's. But, even then, that is not the better way of approaching the sale with customers.

Consider the following example as it relates to an auto-insurance policy. Note how the linking of features to benefits by way of a simple bridging phrase links the discussion of product from the logical, literal side of the left-brain to the emotional, decisive side of the right-brain.

The Feature-to-Benefit Exercise

Left-Brain Language	The Linkage	Right-Brain Language
Factual in Nature	Bridging Phraseology	Emotional in Nature
Features Tell (What It Is)		**Benefits Sell** (What it Does)
1. **Liability Coverage** *Protection that pays the other party for any property damage or injuries that you are responsible for as an at-fault driver.*	"What this means to you is…" "How this helps you is…" "The benefit to you is…" "The importance for you is…	"You'll have the peace of mind and assurance knowing that your family money and assets have a wall of protection about them if you are the at-fault driver in an accident and the other person comes after you for payment, or, worse yet, decides to press legal civil charges against you by suing for damages."

Left-Brain Language	The Linkage	Right-Brain Language
Factual in Nature	Bridging Phraseology	Emotional in Nature
Features Tell (What It Is)		**Benefits Sell** (What it Does)
2. **Medical Payments Coverage** Protection that pays medical bills of the insured and any insured passengers within the vehicle for injuries sustained in an auto accident	"What this means to you is…" "How this helps you is…" "The benefit to you is…" "The importance for you is…"	"You can rest easy knowing that you and your passengers can seek medical care just about anywhere for injuries sustained in an automobile accident, regardless of who is at fault. There's not all the red tape normally associated with stand alone medical insurance coverage. No PPOs or HMOs to hassle with. It covers from the first dollar charged with no deductible to worry over. It's simple, it's easy, and it's a great supplement to any other coverage you may have. Think of it as health insurance for car accidents, but without all of the hassles of deductibles, co-pays and medical preauthorization."

Left-Brain Language	The Linkage	Right-Brain Language
Factual in Nature	Bridging Phraseology	Emotional in Nature
Features Tell (What It Is)		**Benefits Sell** (What It Does)
3. Uninsured Motorist Coverage Protection that pays you for injuries and property damage sustained in an automobile accident where the other party does not have insurance and is the at-fault party.	"What this means to you is…" "How this helps you is…" "The benefit to you is…" "The importance for you is…" "What this means is…"	If you are in a wreck and hurt by an uninsured motorist, which is not as uncommon as some people might think, this protection ensures that you are not taken advantage of by the irresponsible nature of the "other guy" who is at fault and has no insurance to pay you for your injuries. It's an unfortunate reality of the roadway that a high percentage of people driving today do so without insurance. Essentially, what they are doing is telling you to take care of it yourself…and that's not fair to you. This coverage does just that: It protects you if you are injured and prevents you from being taken advantage of by others who choose to not do the right thing."

Customer-Centered Benefit Language Is Powerful Language

The second way of speaking to the customer is "the benefit way." It is a much more powerful way to hold a sales conversation. It is a belief system that strives to communicate to the customer about what the product *does* and *can do for them.* It is the sales philosophy of the left- and right-brain together, where facts, figures, and features are bridges to the emotional reasons for buying. Thus, rational thought and logical validation support the emotional decision to buy.

As someone who works with insurance and financial services every day, I have taken each product offering that we sell and have constructed a *features to benefits* grid so I can connect more readily with people and their emotional centers.

The result for me in constructing and then studying the features to benefit graph was the joy in discovering a new, more effective way of thinking, speaking, and dealing with customers. I got away from being product-focused and concerned about the minutia of features and became more customer-focused and oriented to benefits, which is what customers want and need anyway.

Constructing such a grid and using this methodology of changing how you speak to customers is a simple process, one that is rudimentary in nature—punctuating the fact that it is easy yet effective in changing how sales professionals communicate with customers.

But, as you will discover quickly, it is a very difficult process to put into action if you are rooted in the *old way* of speaking and selling from the left side of the brain. But sales professionals, who were once accustomed to the traditional features way of holding sales conversations, find their sales and client retention increasing as a result of changing how they speak to customers. That change begins with the exercise of translating and communicating features to benefits.

"It is a luxury to be understood."

RALPH WALDO EMERSON

Sales is a contact sport; it is a profession that depends upon effective communication for its very existence regardless of the product or service that is being sold. Therefore, communicating value and helping the customer to perceive the value you are offering is a critical skill for success. Emerson is right: "It is a luxury to be understood" in most situations. In sales, however, it is more than a luxury—it is a necessity.

Value perceived (understood and appreciated by the customer) is value received (effectively communicated by the sales professional and received by the customer). Do not forget that! Thus, it is crucial that the sales professional understand how price and product fit into the whole package of value and how these two components must be communicated in language that helps the customer perceive that value.

We have spoken at length about price and product and how the two are critical components of "value perceived" in The Value Diamond. We have also looked at how both are often presented or spoken of in a company-centered manner that fails to connect emotionally with the customer. And we have noted how we can shift our habits toward a more customer-centered and benefit-rich sales conversation by way of a simple feature-to-benefit exercise. Faithfully apply this thinking into your sales conversations, and customers will respond to you more favorably and you will see your sales numbers grow.

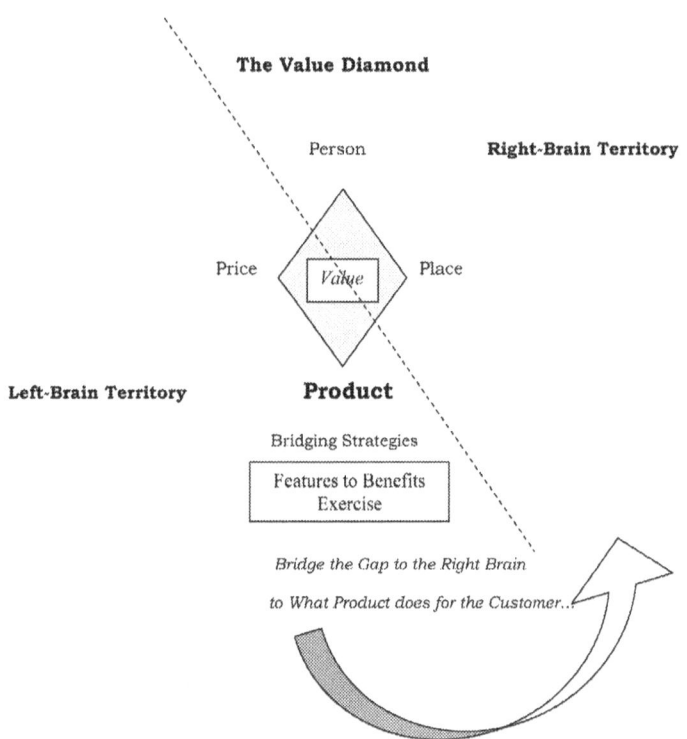

The Value Diamond

Person   **Right-Brain Territory**

Price   *Value*   Place

Left-Brain Territory   **Product**

Bridging Strategies

Features to Benefits Exercise

Bridge the Gap to the Right Brain

to What Product does for the Customer...

Let us examine the other two components of The Value Diamond: the right-brain components of the person (or "sales professional") and the place (the office, website, agency, or store) where selling occurs.

The Person

The *person*, or sales professional, is without question the centerpiece of the entire value proposition for the customer. You are part of whatever you sell. You are the manifestation of the product, the icon for your company or business. You represent everything from quality to reliability.

You are the "difference maker" when customers weigh the value against the price. How you ask questions, what you say in trying to emotionally connect with the customer, and how you look and treat the customer builds on their perceptions of value, worth, and price.

It is the emotional connections that you, the sales professional, make that inextricably tie you to what is being sold. Call it the experience; call it a feeling—whatever it is called it is the person selling that becomes an integral part of why people buy. For this reason, it is important to be measured in how you speak to customers, how you treat them when they come into the office, and how you behave and dress in front of them.

You are the single most powerful component of value in the entire Value Diamond concept. You control perceptions, you communicate value, and you make the product or service you are selling worth it to the customer...or not!

Central to the Lodestar Concept of Customer Connection is the importance emotions play in building customer perceptions of value, particularly upon first meeting someone. Perceptions, no matter how inaccurate, are, in essence reality to the customer. And a customer's reality is the only one that really matters at the point of the sale (People are Judgmental).

Therefore, sales professionals who are careful and sensitive to how perceptions affect the buying habits of people are attuned to make those perceptions as favorable and positive as possible when first meeting individuals. That begins with offering a firm handshake, a friendly smile, a confident look, and maintaining an attentive posture when speaking to them.

People are also naturally *resistant* to the sales process. That resistance is often rooted in fear—fear about what to expect, fear about being pressured into a sale, and fear about the unknown. That is why rapport-building and active listening become such important skill sets to develop and acquire for the person, the sales professional.

People are *egocentric*—they like to talk about what interests them. So give them what they want! You are the only person who can make the sales experience either positive or negative for the customer. Talk about what the customer wants to talk about. Abandon the company-centered language and adopt a manner of speaking in customer-centric terms, terms the customer understands, appreciates, and values.

People are *individualistic*; that is, they desire a buying experience that makes them feel special and not like some number at the deli counter.

More than anyone or anything else, you have the power to impact and influence their emotions and feelings of self-worth. You can make or break their sense of individualism and, thus, make or break a relationship and ultimately a sale.

And, finally, people communicate through an unbroken thread of *visual, vocal, and verbal* elements which form the emotional connective tissue that bridges the left-brain to the right-brain. Each element within that thread possesses its own force to influence and form an emotional connection with the customer. How skilled and effective the sales professional is at weaving this thread can determine whether or not value is perceived.

"Value perceived is value received: This is the motto for the sales professional who strives to sell on value rather than on price.

The Lodestar Concept of Customer Connection

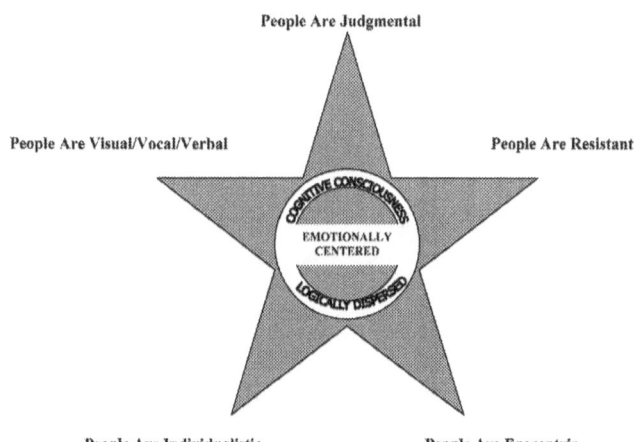

The Lodestar Concept depicts the emotional nature of human beings. It shows how we naturally abound in intuitive sensing, gut feelings, impressions, sensitivities, pride, egotism, likes, and dislikes—the entire gamut of emotions that point to our human makeup.

And it shows for us, when considered in relation to The Value Diamond, that the person, or sales professional, is the one component of the value equation that can stir the entire emotional mix of customer feelings and experiences together to create a sense of value over price.

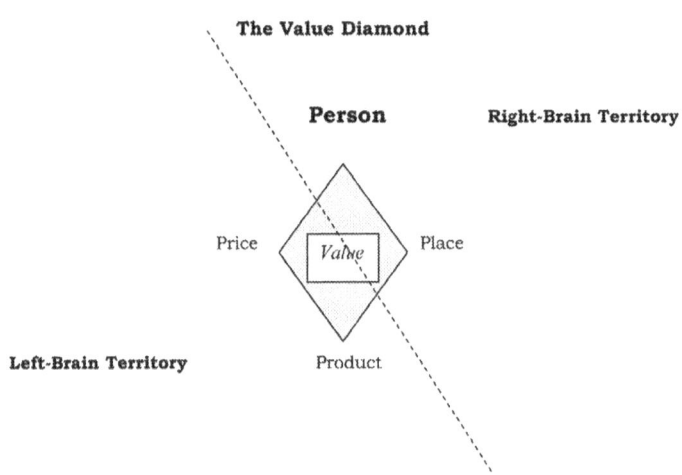

Price and product are naturally understood and appreciated predominantly in the left-brain, the part of our minds that is logical, quantifiable, that puts things into parts and seeks to define, is precise, and exacting. It is not until price and product are linked to the right side of the brain—the conceptual, creative, abstract, visual, emotional side—that they will strongly connect with the customer and become significantly relevant to the decision to buy. That linkage comes by way of the *person* who connects *price* to a value-added statement and translates *product* features into customer benefits.

If price is the *measure* of value and product is the *means* to value, then the person is the *manifestation* of value. You are part of whatever you sell. You are the product, you are the price, and you are the company for which you represent. Sometimes, you are all that the customer knows and sees when it comes to the product or service you sell. Thus, it is critical for sales professionals to learn how to articulate properly and effectively at every juncture of customer contact, whether it is on the phone, face to face, or in a group or seminar setting.

In breaking it down further, there are two areas that are critical to building emotional connection and value perceived in the mind of customers that every sales person must consider under The Value Diamond: *sales strategies* and *marketing strategies*. For each area, I have listed some of the more common activities salespeople (*person*) participate in to grow and retain their customer base while at the same time building value in the mind of the customer.

Remember, these concepts apply to all sales professions regardless of what is being sold. What is presented here does have a direct application to the insurance and financial services industry and an agency/broker distribution system.

Look at each area with an understanding that, although they are systems or activities necessary for any salesperson to be successful, they will only produce better results when consciously employed along with the Lodestar Concept of Customer Connection and the Value Diamond as a basic framework to implementation.

I. Sales Strategies

a. Sales Openings—The first big step toward building value in the customer's mind. *The secret to a strong close is a good opening.* Do not minimize the importance of the sales opening. Work on the following elements of a firm opening:

    i. First Impressions—Develop habits that place you on a favorable basis with people when you first meet with them. Customers are naturally resistant to the sales process. So heed the recommendations of having a good handshake, good eye contact, and a pleasant and warm smile. Break resistance by appealing to the emotionally centered nature of people through The Lodestar Concept of Customer Connection. Get into their world and offer them a token of your gratitude. Utilize the power of psychological reciprocity, which states, "You get what you give." In other words, make sure that you give something to the customer. That gift may be your time or your attention—two things that ought to be an automatic part of your sales conversation strategy anyway. Or, your gift may come in the form of an actual object (e.g., company calendar, mug, pen, book, key chain, et cetera.). Whatever your decision, whatever your gift, it is wise to show kindness and gratitude for the customer investing their time in talking to you about what they want and need. Their gift back to you as a result (reciprocity) is their time and attention. If you practice this habit with people, they will automatically give back in return. Never underestimate the power of hospitality and the desire for people to feel special. Ask yourself, "How can I make the customer's experience a positive one for them when we first meet?" This question, and its answer, forms the sales conversation template for all your strategies and actions.

ii. The Introduction—Establish an agenda with the customer when you first begin to delve into the sales conversation. Introduce yourself, your associates, your company, speaking in customer-centric language ("What this means to you, Mr. Customer, is . . ."). Allay their fears and gain trust by asking questions and showing interest in them. Provide the customer with a brief agenda about what you hope to accomplish and work through together with them at that moment. Ask them questions and tell them what they get when they buy from you. Let them know the value they get by choosing to do business with you.

iii. The Interview—Establish a systematic process of questioning and formulating good open probes. Your level of inquiry into their lives elevates them. It reveals your interest in them and makes them feel valued and special. Get the customers talking about their hopes, dreams, aspirations, concerns, and personal needs. Allow the customer to express themselves and reveal their emotional reasons for why they would buy. Remember, people never really get a sense that they are ever fully listened to in life. Actively listen. Practice exclusive attention with them by giving them your attention and affirming what they are saying. Give them the emotional connection that they want. Translate features into benefits and master the skill of speaking in language the customer understands and relates to emotionally.

iv. Understanding the Value Diamond—Build on your fundamental knowledge of the four components of value and how they form a strong emotional connection with the customer if articulated in customer-centered language. Recognize that we are all wired with a left- and right-brain stimulus and response system. Do not ignore the relevance of the left-brain in bridging the emotional centers of action of the right brain. Also, do not ignore the dominance of the right-brain's emotional centers in being the catalyst for action and deciding to buy over that of the logical left-brain. *Emotional Connection* = *Value*. Thus, imagery, storytelling, metaphors, and the emotional appeals we make directly to the customer as to "why" they should buy become critical to sales success and truly meeting customer wants and needs. *Price* + Emotion = Value; *Product* + Emotion = Value; *Person* + Emotion = Value; and *Place* + Emotion = Value. Sell the whole package.

v. How to Handle Objections—Establish a template that acknowledges customer objections and seeks to uncover the basis for them. Understand what an objection really is when a customer has one. Respect their right and reasons for objecting. Overcome objections with self-discovery questions and revalidation of what was covered during the sales conversation and interview. Make sure that you understand the true emotional reason for why they would buy.

vi. Closing/Asking for the Sale—This is the "when," "how," and "what" to close on when value has been perceived.

Never quote price without connecting it to the emotional reason for buying. Reiterate the emotional reasons for buying that the customer revealed during the interview phase of the sales conversation in order to close strong.

II. **Marketing Strategies** (the systematic activities you execute and the advertising you employ to *get people in front of you* and to *keep people from leaving you*)

a. "Getting People in Front of You"

i. Attraction of new customers through marketing systems such as:

(1) Referral Systems
(2) Outbound/Inbound telephone strategies to get appointments and eventually close sales
(3) Direct Mail activities and follow-up contact strategies
(4) Door-to-door/Direct Contact prospecting activities
(5) Centers of Influence/Key Business & Personal relationship contacts for customer leads
(6) Internet leads generation from company websites and follow-up contact activities
(7) Seminar/group marketing presentations

    ii. Attraction of new customers through advertising such as:

        (1) Billboards
        (2) Internet
        (3) Television
        (4) Radio
        (5) Newsprint/Magazines/Phonebook
        (6) Mailings/Fliers

b. "Keeping People from Leaving You"

    i. Strategies to systematically *cross-sell* other products and services to existing customers to strengthen and solidify the relationship and reduce the likelihood of defection

    ii. Strategies that seek *reasons to speak* and *reasons to meet* with existing customers; the more often you are able to converse with a customer the greater the potential for a deep relationship to be established--this helps to stabilize your customer base

    iii. Strategies that focus on making the customer *feel appreciated and valued* such as a responsive customer service channel, an active customer appreciation system such as "thank you" calls and letters, a sales style that incorporates the tenets of the Lodestar Concept of Customer Connection and sells on the value components of the Value Diamond

c. *Customer Points of Perception* (CPP)—This speaks to every touch point juncture the customer has with your business, whether it is a call-in, walk-in, call-out, seminar situation, or other. The primary purpose is to identify each CPP, prioritize their importance to the business, and formulate strategies that ensure that the customer is getting the experience they expect and deserve. Transacting business is always an emotional experience for the customer.

The Value Diamond

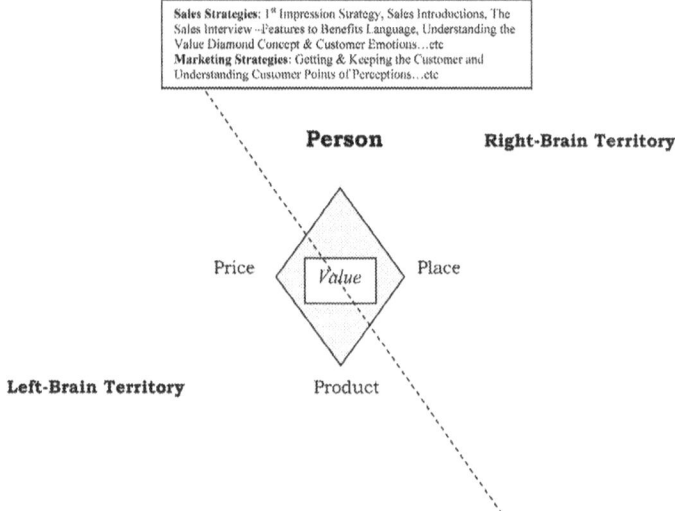

The price is the *measure* of value; the product is the *means* of value; the person is the *manifestation* of value; and, finally, the place where business is transacted is the *source* of value. Let us look at this final component of The Value Diamond.

Price Is the Measure of Value
Product Is the Means of Value
Person Is the Manifestation of Value

The Place

The *place* represents any setting or portal where business is transacted. For this particular discussion, our focus will be on the traditional brick and mortar storefront setting (e.g. insurance office) versus an Internet website, kiosk or some non-traditional *place* where business is transacted. Nonetheless, much of what we will discuss about the place is relevant to these other settings where business is transacted.

There are two aspects of the place that factor into customer perceptions of value: its <u>physical nature</u> and its <u>professional nature</u>.

"How we decorate and present our store...says a lot about the way we feel about our customers and employees. And it tells people what our values are; it's in keeping with the kind of customer we want to attract...If selling is theater, then our selling area is the stage. We use it to set the tone. We want people to walk in and say, "Ooh!"

CARL SEWELL AND PAUL BROWN
CUSTOMERS FOR LIFE[5]

The Physical Nature of the Place

Your place of business reflects who you are, what your values are, and what you think of the business you are in. The physical nature of the place matters greatly because it establishes a tone and an expectation in the mind of the customer about you and how you do business and what experience they can expect to have when dealing with you.

From the moment customers view your place from the street to the first steps they take into the entryway and reception area, customers form perceptions, judgments, and opinions about who you are and how you treat people like them. Remember, people are judgmental in nature, and they are judging you by what your place looks like and feels like to them.

"In the factory Revlon manufactures cosmetics, but in the store Revlon sells hope."

CHARLES REVLON
FOUNDER OF REVLON COSMETICS

So, it is a practical business matter to ask, "Does my place of business accurately reflect who I am?" Or, better yet, "Does the physical makeup of my place of business reflect the things about me and the kind of values that I hold true and want customers to perceive about me? Does my place of business give the customer the emotional experience they are craving?" These are the tough questions that need to be asked if you are to raise the level of your sales production and connect with customers more readily and effectively before your competition does.

Customers respond well to a clean, warm environment that is visually appealing and attractive with easy access and convenient parking. They are looking for a place that is inviting and that is not a difficult place to enter. Comfortable, good lighting and pleasant aromas—or at least the absence of offending smells—enhance the customer experience in a positive way.

There are multitudes of business places that pay little to no attention to such details. Since that is the case, you have a wide open opportunity to differentiate yourself from the competition through acute attention to your physical setting.

The Dentist Office Experience

Not long ago, I went to the dentist for a checkup and cleaning. What should have been a routine exercise for me turned into a negative customer experience that prompted me to seek out and *do business* with another dentist.

To begin with, parking was a problem. Access into the parking lot was difficult. The place—in this case, the actual office—was formerly a home that had now been converted into a place of business. There was a small driveway entryway that ran along the one side of the building to an area in the back set aside for customer parking. I was driving a van.

I turned onto the narrow driveway and proceeded to the back of the building (house) to park. To my disappointment, I discovered that there was very little room to park my van. In fact, there was space for only three cars, maybe four if you squeezed in tightly. And even if I'd gotten into a parking space, it would have been a difficult venture for me to back out after my appointment was over anyway.

I noticed that a large segment of the former backyard was still grass. I remember thinking how stupid and cheap it was that a portion of the yard wasn't converted into parking space. It made sense and could have been done for a nominal amount of money.

So, I decided to park on the street. It was going to be easier in the long run and I could avoid the hassle of being boxed in by another car when I was ready to leave.

So I carefully began to back my van out of the driveway, only to have to hit my brakes suddenly because another customer had decided to pull onto the driveway at the same time. It was a standoff, and it was awkward, inconvenient, and just an all-around hassle for me. After an innocent game of chicken, I managed to negotiate my way around the other car and back onto the street, but not without getting the *evil eye* from the other guy. I found a spot on the street to park just around the corner from the office.

Now with the car parked and worries about re-encountering the parking-lot guy again, I walked toward the office and noticed that the sidewalk and walkway into the building were not cleared of snow. I had dress shoes on and just knew that my feet were going to get soaked from melting snow once I got into the warm office air. Not a good feeling.

The office was a big, two-story building probably built in the 1940s or 1950s. It had the gingerbread trim and large porch area that told you that it was quite a place back in its day. But now it was weathered and in need of a good paint job.

So, again, I thought to myself how cheap the dentist must be...paint is not expensive, and all this place would need is a good coat of it to make it look nice. Did I really want this guy working on my teeth?

Finally, I get into the reception area, the place I think that I can finally stop and sit for a minute to collect my thoughts before actually seeing the dentist. But that wasn't the experience I got. Right when I walked in to the reception area, there was a makeshift 8 ½" x 11" white-notebook-paper sign unevenly taped to the wall that read:

***Do not** be more than 10 minutes late to your appointment or you must reschedule.
***No more than one person** should accompany you in the waiting room area.
***No** cell phone usage.
***No** food or beverages in waiting area.

I was stunned. How cheesy it was to tape a paper sign directly onto a painted wall. It was also cheap and unprofessional. I wasn't feeling "the love," or feeling special, and valued as a customer after reading the sign itself. It was very negative in its tone.

Now, I am sure that if I asked the dentist why he put the sign up he would have a logical explanation for each point. But the fact remained the same; it set a negative tone in the mind of every customer that walked into the building.

And as emotionally centered creatures who buy on emotion and justify with logic, that sign would be the first thing to go if I were in charge of the business. I would then find better, more positive means to get the same message out so my customers would not perceive me as rude, negative, cheap, or unprofessional. Because, perception is reality!

The Professional Nature of the Place and the Unforgivable Sin

Finally, to make matters worse, I approached the receptionist at the counter and said hello, only to be ignored as she held a phone up to her ear. Much in the same way as my previous story of the attorney's rude office receptionist, this particular individual failed to acknowledge me. In turn, she took something away from me that injured my sense of individualism and my need to feel special and important. Rising within me, secretly, was a quiet resentment toward her and the dentist for making me feel this way.

Now I know that she appeared busy, and I will concede that she was likely conversing with a customer on the phone and, therefore, not able to immediately serve my needs. But I would not accept her refusal to acknowledge me and treat me as someone who is of value and worth.

There is an unforgivable sin in the world of business—and in life, for that matter. It is the sin of ignoring someone. She was guilty of it.

To top it all off, after standing there feeling silly and somewhat unsure of my next move, the receptionist finally shows me signs of life by handing me a clipboard with forms and a pen attached to it. She never even looked up at me!

The message was clear by that time. She was telegraphing through body language, "Go sit down, and don't talk to me until you've filled out these forms."

I took the clipboard, turned to sit, and who did I see next to the only open chair in the reception room? Mr. Evil Eye from the driveway standoff!

That was it for me. I put down the clipboard and left, determined to find another dentist who cared about me and didn't make it such a chore for me to see them. The <u>physical nature of the place</u> matters and, from my story, I hope that you sense how the <u>professional nature of the place</u> matters as well.

Keep in mind that I never had the opportunity to meet the dentist personally. But I feel that I did get to meet him through the combined experiences of my parking odyssey, the snow-covered walkway, the paint-starved building, the rude and tacky paper sign, the equally rude receptionist, and the Mr. Evil Eye episode that would have never had occurred if there was adequate parking space.

These are not things that I value or care to experience when buying. So I went somewhere else to spend my money.

It Does Not Matter if Customer Perceptions are Accurate

It Only Matters that Customer Perceptions are Favorable

"Each contact a customer has with a company is a "potential perception point" that influences a customer's judgment (or a series of judgments) about the company. These judgments can be positive, neutral or negative, and add up to a final choice on the part of the customer whether or not to make a purchase from you, the salesperson (and your colleagues, the sales team.)."

DAVID FREEMANTLE
WHAT CUSTOMERS LIKE ABOUT YOU[6]

We are perceptive beings. We pick up signals everywhere we go from everyone we meet. The dentist may have been a good one. He may not have been a cheap person at all. But that is not what his *place* told me.

Signage, parking-lot access, dress, colors, smells, facial expressions, reception areas, greetings, decorations, voices, music, tone, and even sincerity are just some of the things we sense and process from the environment about us...and they tell us if this is a place we want to do business with or not.

Transacting Business Is Never an Emotionally Neutral Experience

Any encounter that we as social beings experience has some emotional charge to it. For the sales professional, it is doubly important to recognize this fact and to create circumstances that are emotionally favorable to the sales process.

Customers crave a good *experience*; they want to *feel* good about buying and transacting business. The place, the actual source or location where the sales transaction occurs, can either create that good experience for the customer or, instead, send them down the street to the competition who will give them what they are looking for.

"Moving toward what makes us feel good and what we like and moving away from what makes us feel bad and what we dislike, is the basic binary code of behavioral choice..."

DAVID FREEMANTLE
WHAT CUSTOMERS LIKE ABOUT YOU[7]

How can we build a value connection that will make customer perceptions about us and our product strong, positive, and alluring to the sale at the *place* where we do business? The answer lies in taking a systematic approach to analyzing every point of contact, or touchpoint, the customer has with a business and then grading the impact and importance it has on the customer's perceptions of value.

Customer Points of Perception (CPP) are all the touchpoints that connect a business to the consuming public. A CPP may be a phone call to or from the business, or it may be a simple advertisement in the local newspaper. Whatever the medium of contact, each CPP paints an image in the mind of the customer relative to the experience.

The entire process of building positive value experiences begins with identifying those CPPs of greater and lesser impact on customer experiences. Using a typical insurance agency business model, the corresponding CPPs can be divided into two major categories: CPPs of a *physical nature* and CPPs of a *professional nature.*

Common Customer Points of Perception for an Agency Business Model

I. Physical Customer Points of Perception

   a. Building Appearance: color, structure, condition, porch, door, steps, entryway, roof, gutters, lighting, fixtures

   b. Landscaping Appearance: trees, bushes, flowers, maintenance

   c. Business Signage: lettering, lighting, size, appearance, condition, color, visibility, readability

   d. Building Access: doorway, walking ramp, condition

   e. Parking Lot: access, available spaces, condition of surface, lines & markings

   f. Exterior Lighting: brightness, sufficiency, condition, appearance

   g. Interior Lighting: brightness, sufficiency, condition, appearance

h. Temperature of Rooms: waiting room, hallways, offices

i. Waiting Room Area: furniture, condition, style, comfort, function, accessibility, size, amenities (such as availability of beverages), windows, temperature, music, flooring

j. Physical Layout of Office: flow, structure, ease of mobility, neatness, privacy, cleanliness

k. Office Décor: cleanliness, neatness, condition, colors, style, paint, carpet, furniture

l. Odors and Noises

m. Restrooms: condition, cleanliness, access, availability

n. Amenities: coffee, magazines, plants

* What does the outside and inside of the place say about you, your values, and what the customer should expect to experience when they transact business with you?

* What do you *want* the outside and inside to say about you and your values? *What steps must you take to gain favorable customer perceptions of you by way of your place of business?

II. Professional Customer Points of Perception

    a. Advertisements and Marketing Materials: appearance, appropriateness, location, size, font, color, accessibility

    b. First-Impression Strategy: demeanor, body language, facial expressions, voice tone-volume-pace, handshake, eye contact, greeting, attention, clothing, cologne/perfume-smells

    c. Incoming-Phone-Call Strategy: the greeting, voice, energy

    d. Outgoing-Phone-Call Strategy: voice, energy

    e. Outgoing Mail: appearance, colors, size, style, font

    f. Sales Interviews: conduct, approach, style, sales interview techniques, voice

    g. Claims Handling Strategy: approach, follow-up

    h. Quick and Convenient Customer Service Response

    i. Complaint Handling Strategy/Apology Strategy

The Value Diamond

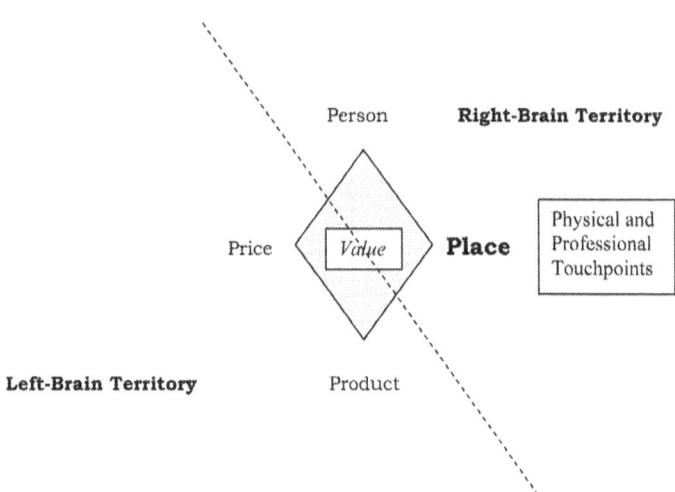

Once a comprehensive listing of CPPs is determined for physical and professional touchpoints, they can each be inserted into a matrix of quadrants that classifies their impact on customer perceptions of value. Impact can be defined in one of three ways: high, medium, and low.

It is a simple process. First, you must determine if a CPP is a physical touchpoint or a professional one. When that has been decided, each CPP is placed into a matrix of quadrants based on their impact potential on customer perceptions of high, medium, or low.

Next, each CPP is evaluated according to whether they *currently* generate a negative or a positive perception in the mind of the customer.

For example, a CPP may be landscaping around your business building that the buying public sees on a daily basis. And it is decided that landscaping is a physical touchpoint with a medium impact potential on customer perceptions of you and the way you do business.

It is further determined that the landscaping is unattractive and over grown, thereby seeding negative thoughts and images within the mind of the customer who sees it around your place of business. As a result, you assess the current impact potential on customer perceptions as negative, thus, identifying an area for improvement so that it can move to the positive column of the matrix.

In their book *Priceless*, Diane LaSalle and Terry A. Britton outline a process similar to this that organizes CPPs and defines customer experiences as *rewards* and *sacrifices* to the business place.[8] They also present compelling arguments on the importance of differentiating one's business by working through what is called an Experience Event Matrix.

The following graphic is an adaptation of their matrix, which I call the Value Matrix. It is a tool that any business can use to help build value through positive customer experiences at the source of value itself: the *place* where business is transacted.

Value Matrix
(Example)

"What is the Customer's Perception?"

Impact	Physical "Touch Points"		Professional "Touch Points"	
High Impact Potential on Customer Perceptions	*Waiting room (Reception Area) *Office Layout * Décor *Furniture *Indoor lighting	*Temperature *Odors *Sounds & Noise *Restroom- clean, neat	* Marketing materials (Personalized Notes, Correspondence & Sales Materials) *Claim Handling Strategy *Complaint Handling Strategy *Incoming Calls	*First Impressions Strategy *Outgoing calls *Sales Interview *Customer Service (Accurate & Timely)
Medium Impact Potential on Customer Perceptions	*Landscaping *Building access *Building Exterior	*Parking access * Outdoor lighting * Outside signage	*Claim Handling Strategy *Advertisements (Radio/Newspaper)	*Advertisements (Television)
Low Impact Potential on Customer Perceptions	*Amenities	*Interior or Color Scheme	*Amenities (Offering amenities-beverages)	*Walk-in Customer Traffic

Negative → Positive   Negative → Positive

The Value Matrix assists the sales professional in systematically grading each touchpoint in the Physical and Professional columns, specifically noting those that create negative or unacceptable customer experiences. Once completed, the CPPs that are identified as needing improvement ("negative") can be prioritized for eventual movement to the positive quadrant after necessary corrections and changes are made.

Each day, businesses are faced with opportunities to deliver rewards to their customers and limit sacrifices that could urge them to go to the competition. In making decisions about design, production, service, distribution, marketing, and many other factors that affect the customer experience, it is critical that sales professionals are aware of the affect those decisions have on the customer's perceptions.

Will interactions with your product, your company, and its staff result in positive or negative experiences? How will customers react to the physical and professional nature of your place of business? Will the events you set in motion represent business sacrifices or business rewards? Bottom line: Are you prepared to deliver a value experience?[9]

"If you don't deliver a Value Experience, your competition will—at your expense."

DIANE LASALLE AND TERRY A. BRITTON
PRICELESS[10]

As emotionally centered creatures, customers determine who they do business with...or who they don't do business with...on an emotional level. The physical and professional CPPs discussed often determine the final outcome of that buying. And since it is clear that emotions are preeminent over logic in the decision-buying process, it is in the sales professional's best interest to understand the impact each component of value has on emotions and how the proper use of each is an inducement to buy and remain loyal.

Otherwise, as the previous quote indicated, if "you don't deliver a value experience, your competition will"! And, worst of all, the competition will deliver a value experience at your expense... literally!

CHAPTER NINE: KEY NOTES

The Value Diamond

* Value is a personal matter—it is defined differently from person to person.

* Value is a perception—it is the union of awareness, understanding, and belief. It is a perception that is controlled by the sales professional to a great degree during the sales conversation.

* Value is measured in terms of *a* price.

* Value is a package—its component parts are Price, Product, Person (the one who is selling), and Place (where the sale occurs).

  1. Commoditization of products is largely an industry creation and not a consumer creation.

  2. 1-800 phone numbers and Internet sites for selling have reduced the value component to a price-only proposition.

* *Price* is predominantly a left-brain-processed component of value.

  1. Price is the quantitative <u>measure</u> of value.

    a. Alone, price is rational, quantitative, factual, sterile, and unemotional. Price is simply a number until it is given relevance.

2. Price gains relevance to the customer when compared to something else.

    a. Too often, the comparison that gives price relevance to the customer is a comparison between your prices to that of the competition's price. If your price is lower, you win. If your price is higher, you lose. That is the logic most sales conversations are based upon.

3. How then should price be presented in order to give it the proper relevance for the customer?

    a. Price should never be presented without it being connected to an emotional reason for buying. Emotions bridge all left-brain thinking to right-brain thinking.

    b. Effective price relevance is achieved by contrasting what you and your company sell to what the customer gets as a result.

    c. A competitor's lower price can only be overcome by your higher value proposition. There is absolutely no other solution to combat a lower price.

5. When should price be presented?

   a. After value has been established, communicated, and perceived by the customer.

   b. Beware...and be ready for the premature price question from the customer. Defer your answer politely until you have been able to establish value for the customer. If the customer insists, give them what they ask for, making sure to connect the price to a commonly held emotional reason for why people buy your product or service.

* **Product** is predominantly a left-brain function.

1. Product is the <u>means</u> of value.

   a. Product features are facts about the product. They are benign, unemotional, and rational, and they connect to the right-brain only through emotional association.

   b. Translate features into benefits in order to speak the language of the customer ("What's in it for me?").

   c. Use the feature-to-benefit exercise's bridging phraseology of "What this means to you is..." in order to bridge the gap to the emotional right-brain, where decisions are made and the impulse to act resides.

2. Value Perceived is Value Received

* The **Person**, or sales professional, is the centerpiece of the entire value proposition for the customer.

  1 The person is the <u>manifestation</u> of value.

     a Humans are social beings that crave emotional connection with other people.

        1.) Consider the lessons from The Lodestar Concept of Customer Connection:

           a.) People are emotionally centered and logically dispersed.

           b.) People are intuitive and emotional when it comes to their impulses to act and decide to buy.

           c.) The person, or sales professional, is the one component of The Value Diamond Concept that can stir the emotions of the customer the most and effectively get them to see the value of owning something over the price to pay for gaining ownership. Thus, the person is the most important component of the entire Value Diamond Concept.

2. The person builds value through emotional strategies:

   a. Sales strategies that bridge the left-brain to the emotional right-brain.

   b. Marketing strategies that bridge the left-brain to the emotional right-brain.

* The **place** is the place of business where the sale is transacted.

1. The place is the <u>source</u> of value.

2. Two elements of *the place* factor into the customer's perceptions of value:

   a. The *physical* nature of the place

      1.) How well does your place of business accurately reflect your values and who you are as a professional?

      2.) How well does your place of business give the customer the experience they are looking for or create a favorable perception in the customer's mind?

   b. The *professional* nature of the place

1.) The unforgivable sin of the business world: ignoring the customer.

2.) It does not matter if the customer's perceptions of your place are accurate; it only matters if they are favorable.

3. How can customer perceptions be made favorable?

   a. Utilize the Value Matrix tool.

      1.) Create a listing of Customer Points of Perception (CPPs)

      2.) Determine which CPPs are of a physical nature, and which ones are of a professional nature.

      3.) Insert them into a Value Matrix based on whether they are of a high, medium, or low impact potential on customer perceptions.

      4.) Then assess whether they are currently impacting customer perception in a negative way or in a positive way.

      5.) Use the results of this analysis to prioritize which CPPs you will correct first...and move to the positive columns of the matrix.

CHAPTER TEN
Conclusion

Sales is a contact sport. It is a fact. We are emotionally centered beings that crave connection with those around us. And, as customers, we bristle with fears, biases, and desires to feel special—all the emotional impulses that make us who we are and drive our desires to buy.

Emotionally centered and logically dispersed is the marquee for how we think and ultimately decide to buy. It is also the standard by which we can measure customers' responsiveness to our sales conversations and presentations. We buy first out of emotion, and then we justify those decisions later with logic. This is a key factor in determining your sales success—understanding and framing your sales strategies around this facet of our human condition will make you a better sales professional.

Contemporary sales thinking and training ignores the fact of emotional centeredness. Most of what is currently espoused by so-called sales professionals is a philosophy rooted in technical jargon with a reliance on models, statistical probabilities, and sales tricks designed to get the customer to buy rather than to get the customer to *want* to buy on their own terms, for their own needs.

Certainly statistical data and other technical information are relevant and important to sales success. But understanding customers and their emotional natures of being judgmental, resistant, egocentric, individualistic, and visual/vocal/verbal is the preeminent skill to acquire as a sales expert.

Understand the customer's emotional nature first and then design your sales systems and processes around it. That is the utility of the Lodestar Concept of Customer Connection and your key to sales success.

Equally important is the need to understand what value is and how it is perceived. The Value Diamond depicts the relationship each component of value—price, product, person, and place—has on the customer's overall perception of value. Customers want value, and if we do not deliver on what they want, they'll go to where they will get it—from the competition!

Therefore, sales professionals must learn to frame their sales conversations so that they bridge the "left-brain" of factual thinking to the emotional side of the "right-brain," the side of our minds where the impulse to act resides. Bridging the two sides of the mind with language that is benefit-rich, following the model of translating features to benefits, and utilizing the Value Matrix are practical ways to make that connection to the emotional mind.

Follow the model of translating features into benefits in all that you say. Ensure your sales conversations are customer-centered, not company-centered, and you will see your sales production increase.

Sales is a contact sport. Now go make contact!

ENDNOTES

Chapter One: The Lodestar Concept of
Customer Connection

[1]   Og Mandino, *The Greatest Salesman in the
World* (New York: Bantam Books, 1974) 52–
53

[2]   David Keirsey & Marilyn Bates, *Please
Understand Me* (Del Mar, CA: Prometheus
Nemesis Book Co. 1978) 3

Chapter Two: People Are Emotionally Centered

[1] Harry Mills, *Artful Persuasion* (New York:
AMACOM, 2000) 106

[2] Daniel Goleman, *Emotional Intelligence* (New
York: Bantam Books, 1995) 6

[3] Mills 106–107

[4] Gerald Zaltman, *How Customers Think* (Boston:
Harvard Business Press, 2003) 8–9

[5] Goleman 31

[6] Scott Robinette, Claire Brand & Vicki Lenz,
Emotion Marketing (New York: McGraw-Hill,
2001) 29

[7] Dale Carnegie, *How to Win Friends and Influence People, Revised Edition* (New York: Simon & Schuster Inc., 1981) 14

[8] Scott West & Mitch Anthony, *Storyselling for Financial Advisors* (Chicago: Dearborn Financial Publishing Inc., 2000) 15–20

[9] Bert Decker, *You've Got to Be Believed to Be Heard* (New York: St. Martin's Press, 1992) 13–16

[10] Carnegie 34

[11] Janelle Barlow & Dianna Maul, *Emotional Value* (San Francisco: Berrett-Koehler Publishers, Inc., 2000) 15

Chapter Three: People Are Judgmental

[1] Daniel Goleman, *Emotional Intelligence* (New York: Bantam Books, 1995) 21

[2] David Freemantle, *What Customers Like About You* (London: Nicholas Brealey Publishing Limited, 1999) 104

[3] Bert Decker, *You've Got to Be Believed to Be Heard* (New York: St. Martin's Press, 1992) 86

[4] Harry Mills, *Artful Persuasion* (New York: AMACOM, 2000) 49

[5] Dale Carnegie, *How to Win Friends and Influence People, Revised Edition* (New York: Simon & Schuster Inc., 1981) 66

Chapter Four: People are Naturally Resistant to the Sales Process

[1] Jacques Werth & Nicholas E. Ruben, *High Probability Selling* (Fort Washington, PA: Abba Publishing, 2000) 3

Chapter Five: People Are Egocentric

[1] Dale Carnegie, *How to Win Friends and Influence People, Revised Edition* (New York: Simon & Schuster Inc., 1981) 54

[2] Susan Berkley, *Speak to Influence* (Englewood Cliffs, NJ: Campbell Hall Press, 1999) 104–105

Chapter Six: People Are Individualistic

[1] Ron Willingham, *The People Principle* (New York: St. Martin's Press, 1997) 15

[2] Dale Carnegie, *How to Win Friends and Influence People, Revised Edition* (New York: Simon & Schuster Inc., 1981) 18–19

[3] David Freemantle, *What Customers Like About You* (London: Nicholas Brealey Publishing Limited, 1999) 38

[4] David P. Snyder, *How to Mind-Read Your Customers* (New York: AMACOM, 2001) 2

[5] Snyder 104

Chapter Seven: People Connect Visually, Vocally, and Verbally

[1] Bert Decker, *You've Got to Be Believed to Be Heard* (New York: St. Martin's Press, 1992) 47

[2] Susan Berkley, *Speak to Influence* (Englewood Cliffs, NJ: Campbell Hall Press, 1999) 4

[3] Gerald Zaltman, *How Customers Think* (Boston: Harvard Business Press, 2003) 38

[4] David Freemantle, *What Customers Like About You* (London: Nicholas Brealey Publishing Limited, 1999) 104

[5] Decker 85

[6] Scott West & Mitch Anthony, *Storyselling for Financial Advisors* (Chicago: Dearborn Financial Publishing Inc., 2000) 16–17

[7] Berkley 2–4

[8] Berkley 5

[9] Freemantle 108

[10] Harry Mills, *Artful Persuasion* (New York: AMACOM, 2000) 93–95

Chapter Eight: Why Buy? Understanding Price and Value

[1] Diana LaSalle & Terry A. Britton, *Priceless* (Boston: Harvard Business Press, 2003) 7

[2] Scott Robinette, Claire Brand & Vicki Lenz, *Emotion Marketing* (New York: McGraw-Hill, 2001) 104

[3] Ron Willingham, *Integrity Selling for the 21st Century* (New York: Doubleday, 2003) 53

[4] Scott West & Mitch Anthony, *Storyselling for Financial Advisors* (Chicago: Dearborn Financial Publishing Inc., 2000) 27

[5] Robinette, Brand & Lenz 30

[6] LaSalle & Britton 5

[7] David Freemantle, *What Customers Like About You* (London: Nicholas Brealey Publishing Limited, 1999) 10

Chapter Nine: The Value Diamond

[1] Mack Hanan & Peter Karp, *Competing on Value* (New York: AMACOM, 1991) 5

[2] Scott West & Mitch Anthony, *Storyselling for Financial Advisors* (Chicago: Dearborn Financial Publishing Inc., 2000) 19–20

[3] Len Serafino, *Sales Talk* (Avon, MA: Adams Media Corp., 2003) 67

[4] Michael E. Gerber, *The E-Myth* (Harper Business, 1986) 91

[5] Carl Sewell & Paul B. Brown, *Customers for Life* (New York: Pocket Books, 1990) 113–116

[6] David Freemantle, *What Customers Like About You* (London: Nicholas Brealey Publishing Limited, 1999) 128

[7] Freemantle 38

[8] Diana LaSalle & Terry A. Britton, *Priceless* (Boston: Harvard Business Press, 2003) 41

[9] LaSalle 43

[10] LaSalle 43

BIBLIOGRAPHY

Barlow, Janelle Barlow & Dianna Maul. Emotional Value. San Francisco: Berrett-Koehler Publishers, Inc., 2000.

Berkley, Susan. Speak to Influence. Englewood Cliffs, NJ: Campbell Hall Press, 1999.

Carnegie, Dale. How to Win Friends and Influence People, Revised Edition. New York: Simon & Schuster Inc., 1981.

Decker, Bert. You've Got to Be Believed to Be Heard. New York: St. Martin's Press, 1992.

Freemantle, David. What Customers Like About You. London: Nicholas Brealey Publishing Limited, 1999.

Gerber, Michael E. The E-Myth. United States of America: Harper Business, 1986.

Goleman, Daniel. Emotional Intelligence. New York: Bantam Books, 1995.

Hanan, Mack & Peter Karp. Competing on Value. New York: AMACOM, 1991.

Keirsey, David & Marilyn Bates. Please Understand Me. Del Mar, CA: Prometheus Nemesis Book Co. 1978.

LaSalle, Diana & Terry A. Britton. Priceless. Boston: Harvard Business Press, 2003.

Mandino, Og. The Greatest Salesman in the World. New York: Bantam Books, 1974.

Mills, Harry. Artful Persuasion. New York: AMACOM, 2000.

Robinette, Scott and Claire Brand & Vicki Lenz. Emotion Marketing. New York: McGraw-Hill, 2001.

Serafino, Len. Sales Talk. Avon, MA: Adams Media Corp., 2003.

Sewell, Carl & Paul B. Brown. Customers for Life. New York: Pocket Books, 1990.

Snyder, David P. How to Mind-Read Your Customers. New York: AMACOM, 2001.

Werth, Jacques & Nicholas E. Ruben. High Probability Selling. Fort Washington, PA: Abba Publishing, 2000.

West, Scott & Mitch Anthony. Storyselling for Financial Advisors. Chicago: Dearborn Financial Publishing Inc., 2000.

Willingham, Ron. Integrity Selling for the 21st Century. New York: Doubleday, 2003.

Willingham, Ron. The People Principle. New York: St. Martin's Press, 1997.

Zaltman, Gerald. How Customers Think. Boston:
    Harvard Business Press, 2003.

About The Author

A dynamic sales coach, speaker, and leader-- Tony Cefalu is a motivator of people and innovator in the field of personal and professional development. An expert in designing and delivering curriculum for a major insurance and financial services company, he is recognized by individuals, sales professionals, and industry peers as a creative problem solver keen on the execution of ideas and delivering concrete results through the pursuit of personal excellence.

A distinguished graduate of the prestigious Air Force Fighter Weapons School and decorated Gulf War Veteran, Tony holds a B.S. from Rochester Institute of Technology and a M.S. and M.A. from Troy State University and Bethany Theological Seminary. A fourteen year veteran of the insurance industry, he also holds the professional designation of CLU.

Tony's blend of academic achievements and real world accomplishments as a salesman, business owner, military officer, world traveler, and professional advisor has helped hundreds of individuals discover new and unique solutions to their own personal and professional growth.

Tony is the founder of Transformation Systems Group, a partnership of consultants and experts dedicated to the development of individuals, small businesses, and organizations looking to discover new capabilities, seize opportunities, and realize their dreams of success.

To schedule speaking engagements and order
additional books, contact the author at
Transformations Systems Group:
www.tdc@transformation-systems.com

TRANSFORMATION
SYSTEMS GROUP

www.ingramcontent.com/pod-product-compliance
Lightning Source LLC
Chambersburg PA
CBHW031959170526
45157CB00002B/469